Edward VI's Lord Chancellor, Richard Rich

Edward VI's Lord Chancellor, Richard Rich

Villain or Loyal Servant?

Laura Adkins

PEN & SWORD HISTORY

First published in Great Britain in 2026 by
Pen & Sword History
An imprint of Pen & Sword Books Limited
Yorkshire – Philadelphia

ISBN 978 1 03611 242 4

A CIP catalogue record for this book is available from the British Library.

Typeset by Mac Style
Printed in the UK by CPI Group (UK) Ltd, Croydon, CR0 4YY.

FSC
www.fsc.org
MIX
Paper | Supporting responsible forestry
FSC® C013604

The Publisher's authorised representative in the EU for product safety is Authorised Rep Compliance Ltd., Ground Floor, 71 Lower Baggot Street, Dublin D02 P593, Ireland.
www.arccompliance.com

For a complete list of Pen & Sword titles please contact:

PEN & SWORD BOOKS LIMITED
47 Church Street, Barnsley, South Yorkshire, S70 2AS, England
E-mail: enquiries@pen-and-sword.co.uk
Website: www.pen-and-sword.co.uk
or
PEN AND SWORD BOOKS
1950 Lawrence Road, Havertown, PA 19083, USA
E-mail: uspen-and-sword@casematepublishers.com
Website: www.penandswordbooks.com

This book is for my darling Tilly,
my star and warrior, who keeps me going.

Contents

Acknowledgements

As always, I wish to thank my parents and those closest to me for their support, encouragement and for simply babysitting while I researched and created this book. There were so many times I wanted to give up, but your support kept me going. Thank you.

To Pen and Sword for having me back to write my second book.

Thanks to Lee-Ann and Charley for your constant encouragement and belief in me.

And finally, to my fellow historians, bloggers and authors who encouraged and supported me before my first book was even thought about, and while writing this one too. For your guidance when I asked for help, and just for being such a lovely online community. I want to thank especially Danielle Burton and Helene Harrison.

Timeline

Date	Year	Significant Tudor Events	Richard Rich
28 June	1491	Birth of Henry VIII	
	1496/7		Birth of Rich
22 April	1509	Henry anointed king	
10 September	1515	Thomas Wolsey becomes cardinal	
	1516		Enters Middle Temple
18 February	1516	Birth of Mary Tudor	
December	1516		Master of Christmas Revels
	1516		Butler and again in 1529
6 June	1520	Field of Cloth of Gold	
	1525		Becomes a reader at the New Inn
	1526		Lost election to become common sergeant
June	1527	Henry starts divorce proceedings against Catherine of Aragon	
	1528		Rich marries Elizabeth Jenks
16 November	1528		Writes to Wolsey with his suggestion to reform the Common Law
December	1528		Commissioner of the Peace, Hertfordshire. Justice of the Peace for Essex
	1529		Elected as an MP for Colchester

Date	Year	Significant Tudor Events	Richard Rich
25 October	1529	Thomas More becomes Chancellor	
December	1530		Commissioner of the Peace for Essex (and again in February 1532, February 1541 and November 1544)
22 March	1532		Appointed Clerk of Recognizances (until 7 Dec 1548)
13 May	1532		Attorney-general for Wales (until 28 June 1558)
16 May	1532	Thomas More resigns.	
25 January	1533	Henry marries Anne Boleyn; his first marriage to Catherine declared null and void	
16 February	1533		Knighted
13 April		Anne Boleyn publicly declared queen	
8 June	1533	Papal authority in England is stopped by order of parliament	
1 July		Henry VIII is excommunicated	
7 September		Birth of Elizabeth I	
10 October			Becomes Solicitor General to Henry VIII (until 13 April 1536)
March	1534	First Succession act is passed by parliament	
April	1534	More arrested and placed in the Tower of London	
3 November	1534	Henry becomes head of the Church of England	
December	1534		Enters the House of Lords

Date	Year	Significant Tudor Events	Richard Rich
	1535	Treason Act passed	
June	1535		Rich visits More and has a conversation which will be responsible for More's execution
1 July	1535	Execution of Thomas More	
27 July	1535		Chirographer, Court of common pleas (until 3 July 1537)
7 January	1536	Death of Catherine of Aragon	
24 April	1536		Appointed the first Chancellor of the Court of Augmentations (until July 1544)
May–August	1536		Senior Knight for Essex and MP
19 May	1536	Execution Anne Boleyn	
30 May	1536	Henry marries Jane Seymour	
9 June-18 July	1536		Elected Speaker for the House of Commons
1 July	1536	Mary and Elizabeth declared illegitimate	
13 October	1536	Uprisings in the north beginning the Pilgrimage of Grace	
25 May	1537		Granted lands held by Syon Abbey around Felsted
February	1538	Pilgrimage of Grace is quashed, and its leaders arrested	
12 October	1538	Edward VI born	
24 October	1536	Jane Seymour dies of perpetual fever	

Date	Year	Significant Tudor Events	Richard Rich
19 May	1539		Rich acquires St Bartholomew's priory, London and converts it into a townhouse
	1539		Groom of the privy chamber
June	1539	The Act of Six articles passed in parliament formally titled An Act Abolishing Diversity in Opinions.	
28 June	1539	Act of Precedence passed	
11 December		Anne of Cleves arrives in Calais	Rich is part of the welcoming committee for Anne
6 January	1540	Henry VIII marries Anne of Cleves	
9 July	1540	The marriage of Anne of Cleves and Henry VIII is dissolved	
28 July	1540	Thomas Cromwell is executed on Tower Hill	
28 July	1540	Henry VIII marries Catherine Howard	
By August	1540		Privy Councillor (until November 1558)
13 February	1542	Catherine Howard is executed on Tower Green	
28 July	1543	Henry marries Katheryn Parr	
24 April	1544		Becomes joint chancellor of Court Augmentations with Sir Edward North chancellor
1 May	1544		Appointed Treasurer for the French War (until December); spends 5 months in France

Date	Year	Significant Tudor Events	Richard Rich
14 July		Henry goes to France	
18 July	1546	Anne Askew is burned at the stake	
28 January	1547	Death of King Henry VIII and ascension of Edward VI	
16 February	1547		Created Baron Rich
23 October	1547		Lord Chancellor
21 December	1551		Resigns office as Lord Chancellor
22 January	1552	Execution of Edward Seymour	
21 June	1553		Signs Edward VI Device for the Succession
5 July	1553	Death of King Edward VI	
9 July	1553	Jane Grey proclaimed queen in London	
18 July	1553	Mary I proclaimed queen	
October	1553		Appointed commissioner of claims for Mary's coronation, made a Privy Councillor and Trier of petitions in the House of Lords
12 February	1554	Execution of Jane Grey	
26 April	1555		Rich establishes a Chantry in Felsted after the death of his eldest son
	1557		Death of Rich's brother Robert
24 June	1558		Received the honor of Rayleigh
17 November	1558	Death of Queen Mary I	
15 January	1559	Elizabeth I is crowned queen	
24 August	1561		Elizabeth I visits Leighs

Date	Year	Significant Tudor Events	Richard Rich
21 May	1564		Creates Felsted school for boys
12 June	1567		Dies at Rochford Hall
8 July	1567		Buried at Holy Cross Church, Felsted

Introduction

The Tudor era boasts many figures that are well known today: King Henry VIII, his daughter, Elizabeth I, the Virgin Queen, her mother, Anne Boleyn, and Henry's five other wives, and Thomas Wolsey, Thomas More and Thomas Cromwell, to name but a few. So much printed work is focused on these people, and others, covering the various events over the course of the Tudor era from 1485, when Henry Tudor claimed victory at the Battle of Bosworth and was declared King Henry VII, through to the death of his granddaughter, Elizabeth in 1603, 118 years later.

There is one man, however, who was involved in the lives of many of those listed above, but who does not have a biography focusing purely on his life. He is known to many historians, and is described as 'one of the most unprincipled men who have ever held the office'[1], a 'Reptilian arch-villain'[2] with a reputation for immorality, finery, double-dealings, and treachery, and a man 'of whom nobody has ever spoken a good word'.[3] The man in question is Richard Rich, Chancellor of the Court of Augmentation and Lord Chancellor to Edward VI.

Rich was born during the reign of King Henry VII, although not much is known of his early years. He became a lawyer and from then forged a career serving his monarchs until he died of old age during the reign of Elizabeth I. What is fascinating is the degree of involvement Rich had in the various events of Henry VIII's reign, and how he survived unscathed when many of his colleagues and supposed friends faced execution, among them Thomas More and Thomas Cromwell.

It was Rich's involvement with Thomas More that was the catalyst for his bad reputation, for it was his testimony that allowed the jury of More's peers to pass the sentence of execution. Many believe Rich's testimony to be false, and he perjured himself to impress the king, and enjoy the rewards that came with it. He allowed an innocent man to go to his death just so he could personally gain from it.

> Hypocrite, perjurer, oppressor and time server, he is without manner of doubt the most despicable man weather sat in the chair of the commons [...] he had part in the fall of Wolsey, death of More, of Fisher, Cromwell, Wriothesley, protector Somerset and his brother lord Seymour of Sudeley [...] a monster in human shape.[4]

His involvement as Chancellor of Augmentations, and his persecution of both Protestants and Catholics, have not done him any favours either. Even his contemporaries did not entirely trust him, though they most likely respected his knowledge of the law and ability to be loyal while it was in his favour to do so. He was shrewd and ambitious, with an ability to follow orders, whether he agreed with them or not

Bad reputation aside, Richard Rich was an intelligent man and knew the law. He was not alone in being a Tudor careerist and in making it his goal to always stay on the right side of the monarch,[5] even if it meant twisting the letter of the law to achieve this. He was a loyal servant, and his survival into old age is proof of this. Others who played similar parts either met their death on the scaffold or were banished from court.

Rich's rise in fortune came at a time when many men of supposed low birth were able to rise into positions of power and wealth. Men such as Wolsey and Cromwell seem to have set a trend that enabled the likes of Rich, and others including Petre, Paget and Paulet, to achieve positions of honour and wealth due to their intelligence and not their social standing[6]. Though disliked, Rich, and others like him, were able to continue to be useful to the monarch, while avoiding the risk of people remembering his humble origins and potentially turning against him, as had happened with Cromwell.

Richard Rich was Lord Chancellor and first Baron Rich during the reign of Henry VIII. Today, he is remembered as being one of the greatest villains of the Tudor period, a reputation he certainly seems to have earned. He was involved in the downfall of Thomas More and Thomas Cromwell. He was one of the torturers of the Protestant martyr Anne Askew, and and also prosecuted Catholic priests for refusing the English Bible. Rising from a lawyer to Lord Chancellor, Rich's wealth grew, as did his status, and he eventually owned hundreds of properties in Essex, becoming even wealthier with his appointment as Chancellor of the Court of Augmentations.

But was he all bad? Towards the end of his life, Rich withdrew from court life and set up Felsted School, which is still active today. This book explores his life, and his involvement in the Tudor courts, and examines, without bias, if Richard Rich really was the villain that history has painted him to be.

The Life and Career of Richard Rich

For a man whose adult life is well documented, Richard Richs' early years are a bit of a mystery. It is believed he was born around 1497 – in Foxe's *Actes and Monuments* he is noted as being 54 years old in January 1551 – but it is not known for certain who his parents were.

Historians document two potential options. One story goes that Rich was born in London, most likely St Lawrence Jewry, around 1496 to Richard Rich, a merchant, and Joan Dingley[1], and was their second son. However, other sources state that he was born in Basingstoke to John Rich of Penton Mewsey, and Agnes, surname unknown[2]. Evidence for this latter claim comes from the will of a John Rich of Penton Mewsey, who died in 1509, in which his son, called Richard, was to be left a house in Islington, on condition that he was obedient to his mother.[3] Further evidence that his father was John Rich of Penton Mewsey comes from the trial, in October 1555, of John Philpot, Archdeacon of Winchester and son of Sir Peter Philpot of Hampshire. He was on trial for being a heretic in the reign of Queen Mary I. John Rich, who seemed to have been present at the trial, was said to have commented that Sir Peter was a near kinsman of his, for which he was sorry.[4] Sir Peter, who could possibly have been a cousin, lived in Compton, not far from Penton Mewsey, thus making the link more likely.

Although it seems unlikely that Rich's parents were Richard and Joan, P. N. Carter, in his biography of Rich on the Oxford Database,[5] claims that it is quite possible Rich may have had links to the Rich family of London, who had been prominent in the mercers company in the fifteenth century.[6] It is on record that a Richard Rich, who was a mercer and was also appointed Sheriff of London in 1441, died around 1463. It is interesting to note that his father, another Richard Rich, who died in 1447, had lands in Essex, including Great Leighs, which Rich would also hold in the 1530s.[7] There was also a London connection with John Rich, who had a house in the area, in addition to Thomas More mentioning that he knew Richard Rich (of whom this book about) in his younger days (More was a born and bred Londoner).

More evidence to support the London connection comes in the form of Rich' s Coat of Arms. Richard Rich's family coat of arms consisted of a red background (gules) with a chevron and three gold crosses pattée (crosses with rounded ends); two on the top half and one below the chevron. In Dagenham church there is a similar coat of arms above a fifteenth-century brass of Sir Thomas Urswyck, whose wife was Anne Rich, daughter of Richard Rich, Sheriff of London in 1441. This coat of arms shows a chevron between three crosses pattée. Under the ruling of the College of Arms, Rich would not have been allowed to have used something so similar to another's, unless there was a family connection. Somewhere there is a possibility that Richard Rich could be a distant descendant of Richard Rich, Sheriff of London.

It is not certain how many siblings Rich may have had, though there is note of him having a brother, Robert, who, on 24 February 1539, was granted messuage[8] in Bucklersbury, in the ward of Cheap, London. The licence, granted by King Henry VIII, was given to Ralph Sadler Esq to transfer to Robert Rich, brother of Sir Richard Rich, the site, which was formally the property of the monastery of St Leonard of Stratford atte Bowe. Not much is known about him other than he died in 1557[9].

In terms of Rich's appearance, we do not have much to go on. The one portrait in existence was done by the famous Tudor artist, Hans Holbein (now in the royal collection: RCIN 912238). The black and white portrait is bust length, with its sitter facing to the right, and was done with chalk, pen and ink. It shows a man looking to one side. He wears a flat bonnet on his head, with flaps covering his ears. Low, flat bonnets were the fashion of the time, with the brim becoming quite plain from the 1530s,[10] which seems to match Rich's hat. His hair is short, which again became the fashion in the 1530s, and he is clean shaven. His clothes are not shown so we cannot comment on his dress from this sketch. His tomb shows him as having a long beard and luxurious robes, but this image was not created in his lifetime, and was most likely an image of what was fashionable at the time.

We can assume that Rich would have worn the best quality clothes, in keeping with this his rank and status. He was most likely a vain man, and would want people to know who he was. But though we can only guess at his style and attire, there are some glimpses we can get from the records. On 28 April 1535 there is an account from Robert Packington, a mercer of London, who had requested payment from Rich for 13yds of 'saye [woollen cloth] black', 2yds of 'bryges satin yellow', 6yds of 'tawney velvet and Sarssenet[11] black'. The following month another order was recorded for '1 roll bock[ram] black,' with a repeat order in August[12].

During the 1520s and into the following decade it was popular for men and women of wealth, such as the gentry and merchants, to wear black. This was because a lot of dye was needed to make black cloth, so it was expensive. As with stately homes, clothes were another way to show off one's wealth. There were even laws passed by Henry VIII in 1533 stating that only those with an income of £40 a year could wear any silk velvet, even a purse or hat, while an income of £200 a year (or status as a knight or the son of a lord) was necessary to wear a voluminous gown of silk velvet.[13] Rich would certainly have been one to flaunt his wealth, and would not have been shy about it.

* * *

Not much is known of Rich's private life. We do know he was a keen gambler, especially at cards. Records show that between 1537 and 1539 Cromwell, who was also a keen gambler, lost almost £50,000 (in modern money), and some of those with whom he played, and probably lost money to, included William Paulet, Sir Richard Rich and the Lord Mayor of London.[14]

Rich married Elizabeth Jenks no later than 1535, although most likely earlier than this due to the dates we have of the marriages of their children.[15] (Their third daughter, Mary, married Thomas Wroth around 1540.[16] The youngest age for a girl to be legally married in Tudor England was 12, so if we take this as the age she was, then her birth would had been around 1528 at the latest). Rich's marriage was, therefore, most likely in the early to mid-1520s, while he was studying at Lincoln's Inn. Elizabeth was the daughter of William Jenks, a wealthy spice merchant, and Elizabeth Adams, born around 1510. It is not certain how the two became acquainted or if it was a love match or one of convenience. Rich would have been in his early twenties and she would have been 18 years old. We do not know much about their relationship, or about Elizabeth. There is nothing noted of any scandal surrounding the pair, unlike some other Tudor gentry couples. We know Rich had at least one illegitimate child, whom he acknowledged, but this is not to say he and Elizabeth were not happy with each other.

A drawing of Elizabeth by Hans Holbein shows the head and bust of a woman, facing slightly to the left. It was most likely done in partnership with one of Rich (no exact date is given on the drawing, but it is thought to have been between 1532 and 1543). Drawn in black and coloured chalk with pen and ink, the sketch measured 37.4 by 30.3 inches and today is in the Royal Collection (RCIN 912271). The woman in the image looks to be middle aged, with a prominent nose and a stern look. She wears a gable hood, which was the style, especially when Catherine of Aragon was queen, and later Jane Seymour. She wears a partlet over a traditional gown of the period, typical of someone of her age and status, which 'would help keep the exposed chest and neck warm as well as be a fashionable accessory to change up the look of a gown. A partlet like this would most likely have been made of black velvet regardless of the colour of the gown.'[17]

Elizabeth gave birth to 14 children between 1528 and 1545:[18] four sons – Hugh, Robert, Nicholas and Edward – and 10 daughters – Margaret, Agnes, Mary, Dorothy, Anne, Audrey, Elizabeth, Winifred, Frances and Barbara. Their eldest son, Hugh, died in 1554, before his father. It would be their second son, Robert, who would be the one to inherit his father's title and estate on Rich's death. Rich was also a father to at least one illegitimate son, named Richard, whom he would recognise him as his son, and even mention him in his will.

In the late 1530s Rich made Leighs Priory his family seat, where he, Elizabeth and his children would reside (until his children were married) . In his various roles, Rich frequently visited London to be present at court and in attendance on the monarchs, though at times he would be further afield, staying in various stately homes, if the king was on progress. Rich also had a home at Rochford Hall, another manor he owned in Essex, and he eventually accumulated a townhouse in London, converted from what used to be St Bartholomew's Priory.

Rich started training as a lawyer and entered the Middle Temple, one of the Inns of Court, in February 1516. This was one of the options for a young man who wished to seek advancement in Tudor England. If it did not necessarily mean it would lead to a career as a lawyer but would at least prepare them for adult life. In fact, it is believed fewer than ten per cent would actually go on to a career in law, most attending just to network rather than having any intention to practise law.

Sometimes referred to as the 'Third University' of England, the Inns of Court were, in effect, universities for the laity, and were thought to have had more of an influence on the students' life than that of Oxford or Cambridge at the time. Those wishing to become the best lawyers would enter one of the four Inns of Court in London, where they would study for up to 20 or more years at a time. There were six classes of common lawyer: serjeants and judges, clerks and office of the central court, attorneys, apprentice, barrister, solicitor and accounts. The highest rank of their profession would be that of Sergeant at Law. The legal profession was a significant element of late mediaeval England society, not only due to its intellectual contribution to the development of England's institutions, but also because of the opportunities it provided for gifted individuals to rise and prosper[19].

In addition to learning the law, students would learn to sing and dance and acquire a form of 'liberal education'. While studying, Rich and his peers would be introduced to the names and people who would matter and who would go on to carry positions of power. Not only would they study alongside one another, but they would also dine with them, drink, and socialise, as one would expect university students to do today when staying in their halls of residences. Bonds would be made to last a lifetime.

However, not all those who entered the Inns would stay lawyers. Some would become civil servants, while for others it was more an education to enable them to manage their finances and investments, and bring them into contact with a network of men whose alliances, friendships and even marriages (if there were females in the families) could be forged. The opportunity to network among the future politicians of the country would have been a strong temptation for anyone wanting to advance themselves and their families, especially a man such as Richard Rich.

Like all the students, Rich slowly climbed his way up in the court. Students were first involved in basic reading of the law and rote learning, and in disputations or moots at an elementary level. When he was of sufficient standing to dispute at or outside the 'bar' of his inn, he became an under barrister. Later, he might be chosen to deliver lectures, and in the capacity of lecturer, or 'reader', he also presided over disputations. After reading, he became a senior member of his inn, sitting on the bench at moots.[20].

According to the honourable Society of the Middle Temple he was appointed 'Butler for Christmas time' in 1516 and by 1525 he became a reader at the New Inn (a window in the hall there bears the inscription '*Ricardus Rich dominus cancellarius Anglie lector*'[21]), and in 1529 he was appointed autumn reader. A reader in the Inns of court was appointed to give a series of lectures on a particular topic to the students. They would usually serve one year and be a member of standing at the court. The practice of reading at the court was done twice a year, at Lent and in the autumn, when Rich was appointed. The event would take place over a few years and could expound upon a particular statute, and disputation and discussion of sample cases would follow. As with all Tudor events, the reading would end with a grand feast, usually at the reader's expense. For Rich to have been appointed a reader shows the status and respect he was already achieving amongst his contemporaries, and how he took his education seriously. Whatever he decided to do later in life out of greed, initially he acted out of passion in the law (much like Thomas More).

By 1526 Rich decided to expand away from the Inns of Court. He applied to be the Common Sergeant for the City of London, a role of considerable status which dates back to 1291. He was unsuccessful and the appointment went to William Walsingham, who was the Crown's nominee.

His hard work did eventually pay off when he was appointed as a Justice of the Peace for Essex and Hertfordshire in December 1528. This appointment may have come about due to the involvement of Cardinal Wolsey, from whom Rich had sought favour in 1528. Rich had reached out to Wolsey on 16 November 1528, suggesting a reform of the Common Law:

> Knowing Wolsey's great zeal for the reform of the common law, which, however, he is too busy to attend to, begs to be called before him so that he may declare the abuses that are daily used, and suggest remedies. Wishes to be heard in private before anything of this matter gets abroad[22].

At the time Wolsey did not act on Rich's suggestion, most likely as he was occupied with the king's divorce from Catherine of Aragon, but it may have brought him to the attention of Wolsey, who knew the worth of a person and their hard work and knowledge. In the following December, Rich was placed on the Commission for the Peace in Hertfordshire, and in February 1529 was made a Commissioner of Sewers.

In November the same year he returned as one of the Burgesses of Colchester to the 'reformation' parliament, which sat from 1529 to 1536.[23] In June 1530 he was placed on the Commission for Gaol delivery at Colchester Castle,[24] and in July was one of those appointed to make a return of Wolsey's possessions in Essex, along with Robert Norwich, Thomas Audley and Thomas Bonham.[25] This involved taking stock of any possessions and landholdings Wolsey had in Essex and documenting them for the king so that he could see how much richer he now was (for example, Hampton Court was a readymade palace for the King to now move into, and of far better quality than his crumbling Westminster).

As a Justice of the Peace, Rich would be one of many appointed in various counties. He would fulfil the role numerous times in his life: in December 1530, February 1532, February 1541, and November 1544, and for St Albans in February 1540. He was on the Commission of Sewers for Essex (responsible for investigating flood defences and drainage of land in a specified area) in January 1540 and 1541.[26]

Justices of the Peace were first mentioned in the reign of Edward III (1327–1377), when an act was passed in 1327 stating that every county needed to have assigned Justices of the Peace:

> [lawful men] in every County of England shall be assigned for the keeping of the Peace, one Lord, and with him three or four of the most worthy in the County, with some learned in the Law, and they shall have Power to restrain the Offenders, Rioters, and all other Barators, and to pursue, arrest, take, and chastise them according their Trespass or Offence; and to cause them to be imprisoned and duly punished according to the Law and Customs of the Realm.[27]

Justices of the Peace were basically responsible for maintaining law and order in their respective counties and were nominated by the Crown. They were usually men who had a good reputation of maintaining the peace, and were usually from the landowning classes, with some being nominated due to their high offices in court (more of a show title than one which involved enacting the role). Though an unpaid role, it had its rewards. Being a Justice of the Peace meant becoming an influential and respectful figure in the county, with an involvement in local politics. It could be a stepping stone to other high positions through links with the powerful figures who ran the country, leading to patronage, and maybe even marriage prospects for family members. After all, these were men who would know more about the goings-on in their localities than lords and nobility, who tended to spend most of their time near the king[28].

Although there was no clear definition of the exact roles and responsibilities of a Justice of the Peace, there were a number of acts that mentioned their powers and what they could and could not do. By the time of Henry VIII's reign, and the changes in how the country was run, the JPs' workload increased even more. This would be beneficial for people like Rich as it allowed them to gain more experience and influence in their locality. The king needed the JPs on his side and made sure they were looked after. This was another opportunity for Rich to progress his career and move towards serving the king directly in court rather than from afar in Essex, and he could use his role as a JP as proof of his loyalty to Henry.

Overseeing the serving of justice being served and deciding on suitable punishments were important parts of a JP's role. Henry, Earl of Essex, wrote to Rich and another JP, Thomas Nyghton, in October 1536: 'causing certain persons accused of robbery begs they will take the advice of Mr. Yngelffeld. Desires one of them should be sent to the Tower, and so handled that the truth may be known.'[29] (Basically, wanting them to at least take one of the accused to the Tower of London and questioned to uncover the truth.)

In 1532 Rich was appointed to the Office of all Recognizances of Debt. He would be paid 3s. 4d. for the making, writing, and enrolment of every such recognizance, and 20d. for the certification of the same.[30] The Clerk of Recognizance was a royal officer responsible for agreements between the Crown and a person to appear in court. They would write up the terms of the legal agreement – recognizance – as well as decide on the penalties for not adhering to it.[31]

* * *

During his early years Rich came to the attention of Thomas Audley, a supporter of Wolsey, MP for Colchester, and Justice of the Peace. The two became acquainted and a friendship developed which continued throughout their adult life. It was through Audley's connections that Rich was given the introductions he needed to enter into the life of the court.

Audley and Rich would have very similar careers. Thomas Audley, born in 1488, was from an old family based in Essex. Where Audley would be rich's stepping stone to the corridors of power, for Audley it was the Duke of Suffolk, Charles Brandon, a close friend of the king, who gave him his entry into the Tudor Court by introducing him to the king. Audley was then made Speaker of the House of Commons in December 1529. From that point he focused on serving the king and proving himself to be a man whom Henry could trust and rely on. It would be Audley who replaced Thomas More as Chancellor after his execution in 1535, making him the first layman to be resident on the King's Council. Audley was eager to please his king, as well as advance his own path to power and position. Unlike More, Cromwell, Brandon and others, Audley did not have a personal friendship with the king, which is, perhaps, what saved him – and possibly what protected Rich.

* * *

It could be said that Rich entered political life in 1536 when he was appointed Speaker for the House of Commons. This appointment seems to have divided opinion, however, as it took the House a few days to authorise him as speaker.[32] The suggestion most likely came from the king, with the house debating if Rich was suitable. Could this be an early sign of a mistrust of Rich or just down to his suitability for the role? We will never know but it is interesting to note.

The role of Speaker dates back to 1377, though a similar role was in existence before that. The Speaker was meant to be the king's spokesperson and to relay information from parliament to the king and vice versa. This meant at times finding themselves a target of the monarch's wrath if things didn't go their way. They were expected to keep order in the Commons during debates. By the time Rich became speaker, no fewer than seven of his predecessors had faced beheading.

It is possible that his appointment at the request of the king came about through the influence of others such as Audley. It is thought that the king may have been advised that Rich was the man who would 'guide the commons though its business, in the direction … [he wanted]'. Rich grabbed his opportunity, aware of the chance to be close to the king's ear, and to get into his good graces through flattery. He compared the King to 'Solomon for prudence and justice, to Samson for strength and bravery, and to Absalom for beauty.'[33] Equally extravagant was his concluding address, likening the king's care for his subjects to 'the sun's influence upon the world'.[34] Even by Tudor standards this was excessive.[35] He was paid the customary fee of £100 as Speaker.[36] Although being close to the king had its advantages, it was not the only source of power. Being a member of parliament also brought influence. The Tudor parliament, although very different from what we have today, was an active body of men who primarily made laws and granted taxation. They discussed the king's requests, and could even oppose them if they felt they were not just. Though the monarch was the head of state, and MPs were an instrument of the Crown first and foremost, they also saw it as their duty to question anything that might impact their individual rights and vote accordingly. Because most MPs looked out for themselves, when they did happen to disagree with the king, certain inducements were put before them to make them more amenable to his requests.

The House of Lords, established in the eleventh century, consisted of members of the nobility, referred to as Lords Temporal, and high-ranking members of the clergy, referred to as Lords Spiritual. The Commons, established in the fourteenth century, was composed of elected members of the knights of the shires and burgesses. There would usually be around 90 knights, two from each shire. Most of those who sat in the Commons were usually placed in their positions by those in the Lords and therefore could easily be influenced. The Lords were usually men of higher standing, and, in some cases landlords: in other words, people who needed to be kept happy. The person who sat at the head of all of this was the king, and he would have the final say on all bills and legislation. England was his empire, and he was its emperor.

* * *

As Rich's career slowly progressed, he found himself in the Tudor Court itself, where the power really lay. It was a mixture of those who held positions of power through their own abilities, and those whose power derived from family ties and from friendship to the king. Rich knew that it was the king and the king alone who held the power and could make or break people's careers, not the various factions and alliances that came and went. However, Rich was also clever enough to know he needed allies. He needed to build so-called friendships with those around him in order to survive in the court, especially with those in higher positions who could help advance his career.

The main person Rich needed to keep on the right side of would be the king. Access to the monarch was crucial for any man wishing to prosper in court, and this was especially true with King Henry VIII. The more astute members of the court soon realised that if they were able to speak with the king one to one, they were more likely to be listened to. After all, a good king would seek and listen to the advice given by his counsel and those closest to him. When Rich first met King Henry VIII, he was not the fearsome tyrant some think of him as today. Henry was 18 years into his reign and had a problem in seeking to divorce his wife, Catherine of Aragon. The Pope had refused to allow it, and Catherine was not budging.

* * *

Henry Tudor was born on 28 June 1491 at Greenwich Palace. He was the second son of King Henry VII and Elizabeth of York. Their eldest was Arthur, born 1586; then Margaret was born in 1489 (future Queen Consort of Scotland); Elizabeth (died as an infant); Mary was born in 1496 (future Queen of France); Edmond was born in 1503 (died as a baby); and Catherine was born in 1503 (died as a baby). Spoilt and knowing his importance from an early age after the death of his older brother, young Henry was raised under the control of his father and grandmother, Margaret Beaufort. He soon became an extravagant and selfish man when he became king. He married his brother's widow, Catherine of Aragon, after falling in love with her as a teenager.

His aim on assuming the throne was to erase the bad memory of his father. He wanted people to think him a fun and lively king, and associated more with his maternal grandfather, King Edward IV. Henry did have good business acumen at the start of his reign and was quick to grasp the functions of government. Although he allowed others to do his bidding, he was very much in control of what was going on. He was quick to disassociate himself from anything that went wrong, laying the blame on those ministers who were actually doing his bidding. He may have learned to do this early on in his reign when it was clear that two of his father's ministers, Edmund Dudley and Richard Empson, were despised of as greedy, power-hungry men who were low-born royal officials in positions of power. Although they were most likely following the king's wishes, many had begun to turn against them and they became scapegoats for the unpopular financial choices made by Henry VII.

On succeeding his father, King Henry VIII, was swift to act against Dudley and Empson. He had them charged with 'constructive treason'[37] and they were executed on 17 August 1510. This move could be seen as a bid for popularity; a power play by the new young king in an attempt to disassociate himself with some of the negative aspects of his father's reign. Such an act so early in his reign displays a cruel and ruthless streak in the king,[38] and it was certainly not the last time he would use scapegoats when things went wrong.

Henry believed, and expected others to believe, that the king was the sole font of power. He was anointed by God, and therefore his wishes would prevail, or there would be consequences. In his early years as king, he sought companionship with the men close to him, and he considered them trusted friends. However, his character would change, and with it his view of the men around him. The early 1530s brought about many changes in the country: the break with Rome; the Act of Supremacy; his divorce from Catherine of Aragon; the dissolution of the monasteries. The executions of Thomas More and Anne Boleyn brought about a change in the king, and in his relationships, as did his jousting accident, which impacted on him physically as well as psychologically:

> Henry did undergo a change and although this was part of a cumulative process it was greatly accelerated by the events of 1536. The damage this year made to Henry's physical and, less tangible, his psychological health appears to have started a chain reaction, tapping into his propensity for high self-regard.[39]

Henry would always remember those around him who did him favours and had his back. Although he allowed some men to rise more than they were due, he would only do so to profit himself. And he knew he could always take it away, especially from those who rose too high. For those who grew close to the king, their stars could shine brightly, but they were also the ones whose fall could be quick and painful. Henry felt betrayal on a personal scale, and would retaliate by executing those who had hurt him the most; at times without legal cause. In total some 68 people were condemned without trial by common law, with 34 being executed. Many of those were condemned through Acts of Attainder due to the fact that they had not clearly committed treason but the king felt that they had.

A few members of Henry's court who survived his reign, like Richard Rich, were those who grew close to the king without becoming personal friends. Perhaps they understood what More was advising Cromwell about advising the king without revealing what it was possible for him to do:

> Master Cromwell, you are entered into the service of a most noble, wise, and liberal prince. If you follow my poor advice, you shall, in your counsel-giving unto his grace, ever tell him what he ought to do, but never what he is able to do [...] For if a lion knew his own strength, it was hard for any man to rule him.[40]

* * *

The royal court was a microcosm of the wider world; everyone knew their place and duty as designated by God. It was what allowed the world to function and peace to be kept. The men who surrounded the king would be classified as the nobility, those who held rank and title, usually inherited by their birth (like Thomas Howard, 3rd Duke of Norfolk), or in other cases created by the monarch as a reward for services rendered (like his childhood friend Charles Brandon who was created Duke of Suffolk in 1514). The nobility consisted of men of learning and supposed wisdom whose wealth enabled them to devote their life to government and the general welfare of the rest of society. Their duty was to rule the lower classes and this sense of superiority at times may have gone to their heads, justifying their power and privilege. This was, after all, how society and the world worked, and though it seems strange to us today, it was accepted. Everyone knew their place.

Although they were of a high rank and class, the nobles still sought favour from the king and would often compete for his ear. Henry was well aware of this, especially later in his reign, and would at times play the nobles off against one another. This helped to make the court into a compliant instrument of his rule. Also, if they were busy competing amongst themselves, it would, in theory, prevent any of them considering opposing the king directly. (There were some nobles who held royal Plantagenet blood, some of whom would become an issue for Henry while others tried to forget their ancestry, knowing this was best means of survival).

* * *

Rich became a member of the new nobility of Tudor England when he was knighted on 12 June 1536. He was now considered part of the gentry, a new class of men who had good breeding but were not considered noble. They may have married into nobility and risen in rank, or they may have had more wits about them than those of noble birth, having had to rise in the ranks purely through their own wits and intelligence, who came from nowhere and made something of themselves. Others would include the younger sons of the nobles, rich merchants and lawyers. They sat just below the nobility but above the middle classes in the social hierarchy, and could survive by transferring their allegiances when it suited them. The gentry were also responsible for local administration, issuing justice in all but the most serious criminal offences, as well as representing the landed interests in government.

As members of the gentry were not as high ranking as the nobility, they needed assistance if they wished to climb higher in society. It was normal for many to seek patronage of someone in a higher position. This allowed for introductions to be made, alliances forged, and even advantageous marriages. Patronage worked at all levels of society not just for the gentry.[41] In some cases, as with Richard Rich and Audley, the one seeking patronage could, in years to come, be sought for patronage themselves. Rich managed to reach the upper levels of the Tudor nobility, ending up in a position where he could return the favour to those who had helped him.

However, the higher one went in society the bigger the fall, and the highest position in Henry's court was to be considered a friend to the king. Those who had risen from the lower ranks, men like Rich and Cromwell, risked being disposed of by those who were already in the higher social ranks. If there was a chance to knock them down a peg or two, it would be taken. This game of politics in the Tudor court was often a matter of life and death, and ended badly for those who had allowed themselves to become close to the king and disappointed him.

Rich entered the court of Henry VIII before this pattern emerged, and as his power and influence grew so did his knowledge of the king. He knew his duty was to serve the monarch, but not to shine too brightly. In 1533 he was appointed Solicitor General, one of the law officers of the Crown, second only to the Attorney General (the chief legal advisor to the king). The appointment was most likely due to the involvement of his former patron, Audley. The Solicitor General was expected to advise the king and parliament on legal matters. Both the Attorney General and Solicitor General were seen as representatives of the Crown and therefore never fully trusted by the House of Commons.

In his capacity as Solicitor General Rich was sent to Kimbolton Castle in January 1536 to take an inventory of Catherine of Aragon's goods after her death. Rich saw an opportunity to use his legal skills and knowledge to the benefit of the king. He would instruct Henry how he could claim her property even though, under the eyes of the law, he had divorced her. She was a widow (of Henry's brother, Arthur) and therefore her goods were hers to leave to whom she wished, not the property of Henry. Rich explained to Henry that he could still claim her goods without acknowledging his marriage to her.

> Pleasing your Majesty to be advertised of my poor mind [...] for I mean none other, but to declare to your Majesty the truth: affirming to your Highness, that I shall be as ready to execute your Graces commandment, according to my most bounden duty, with as much good will, heart, and mind, to my little power [...] Pleasing your Majesty to consider, that the Lady Dowager was a

> sole woman; having by all laws a full authority and capacity to have property in goods and chattels: albeit her Grace affirmed, that all was yours [...] I dare not speak precisely. The full and determinate solution of that question I remit to your Majesty, and to others of your Graces Council, to debate and determine. And therefore in this wise to take and seize Grace's goods as your own, is repugnant to your laws; and, as I think, with your Grace's favour [...] I think you may have, take, and seize the goods and chattels of her by another mean lawfully; which is this: if your Graces pleasure be so, ye may cause a letter to be written to the Bishop of Lincoln, commanding him to grant the administration of all such goods and chattels as lately were the Lady Dowagers, to such as your Highness shall name. And then to have the goods of them to your Grace's use, in recompence of such sums and debts, as your Highnes hath, or shall ley out for her burial, or otherwise. And this, as I think, were the best way, and concurrent with your Graces laws. From Kimbolton, this present xix day of January: by your Grace's Most humble servant.[42]

Rich had explained to Henry, without telling him what he should do, how he could have her goods. For although Catherine of Aragon believed she was still Henry's wife and left her goods to him, under Henry's laws she was not. By requesting the items be left to him from the Bishop of Lincoln as cost of her burial he was not making himself look like a fool. This suggestion from Rich was certainly a good move on his part, and Henry would have certainly appreciated a man with his thinking, a man who was looking out for Henry and no one else.

Other events in which Rich played a part as Solicitor General included persecuting those who were against the king's marriage to Anne Boleyn and the royal supremacy. This included writing the indictment against Elizabeth Barton,[43] and the examination of the Priors of Bevell in Nottinghamshire, and of the Charterhouse in Axholme, Lincolnshire, who refused to accept the king as supreme head, in addition to the arrest of More and Fisher.[44]

Rich would work alongside Audley in the House of Lords drafting bills, including the one creating the Court of Augmentations,[45] where Rich would soon find himself appointed as Chancellor. He was also one of those responsible for persecuting those who opposed the Act of Supremacy, which caused much discord within the country and led to the eventual arrest and execution of Bishop Fisher and Thomas More. He examined those accused in private before either public hearing,[46] which led to More's execution. It is Rich's part in this which has led to his reputation as a 'dastardly […] obnoxious, amoral, ruthless chancer,'[47] who climbed high on the bodies of those more principled than himself.

The Trial of Thomas More

Richard Rich' s role in the trial of Thomas More, which led to his execution, seems to be one of the key moments that led to his reputation as a villain. Did he turn against More for his own gains? Was he following Thomas Cromwell's orders, or even the king's, to achieve what they ultimately wanted. And did Rich's role actually lead to More's execution or was it a foregone conclusion?

Thomas More was born on 7 February 1478 and was educated at one of the best schools of the time. In 1490, at the age of 12, he became a household page to John Morton, then Archbishop of Canterbury. From there he entered the world of the Tudor court, though not before studying at Oxford for two years, followed by legal training to become a lawyer, firstly under the Inns of Chancery and then Lincoln's Inn from 1496 until 1502. More married Joanna Colt, and, after her death, married Alice Middleton. He had four children, all of whom were well educated, which was rare at that time. By 1519 he was secretary to King Henry VIII, which involved welcoming diplomats to court, drafting official documents, and attending the Star chamber. He was appointed Speaker to the House of Commons in 1523. When Cardinal Wolsey fell from the King's favour in 1529, More was appointed Lord Chancellor in his stead, the highest government minister in England.

Lord Chancellor was the highest official role for 'equity and common law, including contracts and royal household cases, and some misdemeanour appeals,'[1] and More excelled at it. As Chancellor he held custody of the great seal and stood at head of his own cabinet of ministers. The role also encompassed being part of the Court of Chancery, which had discretion to mitigate the harsh effects of rulings emanating from common law courts. This has led to the unofficial term of the Chancellor being the 'Keeper of the Royal Conscience'. The Chancellor was the most senior judge in the land bar the king.

On 16 May 1532 More stepped down from his position as Lord Chancellor. He could not reconcile his conscience with his ability to serve the king as Lord Chancellor. More was not alone among those in positions of power and authority who were shocked by the king's break with Rome. They saw it as their duty to serve both the king and the Pope. Now their king had proclaimed himself head of the Church, thus rendering the Pope's authority null and void. Though shocked, however, many took the Oath of Supremacy, some believing their overriding duty was to the king, while others did it merely as an act of survival. More, however, could not accept the king's terms. Although he acknowledged Henry's divorce, he would not take the Oath, and so resigned his post. Initially, Henry had accepted this, but More's continued refusal to accept the Oath irked the king, until he had him placed under arrest.

In 1529 the king had parliament reinstate the charge of praemunire, making it a crime to follow the authority of anyone outside the country, namely the Pope. Despite the Act of Supremacy, More acknowledged the Pope as head of the Church, and therefore superior to the king in matters of religion. It was this reinstatement of the praemunire which persuaded bishops to sign and acknowledge Henry as Supreme Head of the Church of England. The vast majority of the population also felt it best to stay on the right side of the king rather than risk losing their life. Although the bishops only agreed to the passing of the Act of Supremacy after adding 'as far as the law of Christ allows', this was not enough for More and he resigned his post.

Around 1525 a woman named Elizabeth Barton (sometimes referred to as The 'Nun of Kent', 'The Holy Maid of London', or 'The Holy Maid of Kent') started claiming to have prophesied about the future. In 1533, during the Dissolution and Henry's divorce from Catherine of Aragon, she claimed to have visions showing if Henry continued with the divorce and married Anne Boleyn he would not live much longer. Unsurprisingly, this did not go down well with the king when the news was relayed to him, and she was arrested in November 1533 on the charge of treason. Following her charge, in February the following year, a bill was drafted which identified Bishop Fisher, Thomas More, and 11 other supporters, as being her accomplices and conspiring with her. Although More had met with Barton, he had certainly not conspired against the king. He penned a letter to both Cromwell and

Henry on 5 March 1534 stating his loyalty to the king and denying any involvement with Barton[2] (More's name was added to the list conspirators at the last minute at the insistence of the king). Barton was sentenced to be hanged at Tyburn on 24 April, and on the scaffold she declared her prophesies were false and had been made up. As for More, he was safe from the scaffold for the time being, his continued silence on the matter of Henry's marriage to Anne placed him in a precarious position.

Shortly after sending his letters to the king and Cromwell, More was called to stand before the King's Commission in the Star Chamber (which included Audley, Cranmer and Cromwell). He was questioned once more about Elizabeth Barton, and about the king's marriage to Anne Boleyn. On 12 April, while leaving a service at St Pauls, More was handed a summons to appear at Lambeth Palace the following day to take the Oath of Succession.[3] He knew his time was up, and on returning home he informed his family that he would soon be imprisoned, and he attended the summons by the Commission at Lambeth Palace the following day, 13 April. He accepted Anne as queen but once again refused to take the oath, stating that he would not speak against it. But this wasn't enough. He he was placed in the care of the Abbot of Westminster for four days before entering the Tower of London and imprisoned in the Bell Tower.

While imprisoned in the tower, More's friends and colleagues, including Cromwell, continued to try to save his life. Several attempts were made to get him to swear the oath, including by his own family, but More continued to stay silent on the matter. While in prison, at least to begin with, he was allowed some comfort, including access to pen and paper. He completed a book entitled *A Dialogue of Comfort Against Tribulation,* along with letters to his family, including a letter to his daughter Margaret explaining his choice:

> If I had not been, my dearly beloved daughter, at a firm and fast point, (I trust in God's great mercy) this good great while [...] so grievous unto me, as to see you, my well beloved child, in such vehement piteous manner labor to persuade unto me, that thing wherein I have of pure necessity for respect unto mine own soul, so often given you so precise answer before. Wherein as touching the points of your letter, I can make none answer, for I doubt not but you well remember, that the matters which move my conscience (without declaration

> whereof I can nothing touch the points) I have sundry times showed you that I will disclose them to no man [...] my former answers to hold yourself content. A deadly grief unto me, and much more deadly than to hear to hold yourself content [...] For surely if his Highness might inwardly see my true mind such as God knoweth it assuages his high displeasure [...] I can no further go, but put all in the hands of him, for fear of whose displeasure for the safeguard of my soul stirred by mine own conscience.[4]

In response to More's continued stubbornness, it was decided to make things more uncomfortable for him, in the hope of forcing him to change his mind. Whether this came from the king directly or from Cromwell is not clear. In June, Rich was sent into More's cell to remove his writing materials and book. Rich was accompanied by Sir Richard Southwell (who had previously tutored Cromwell's son and been assisted by Cromwell when he and his brothers had murdered another courtier) and a Mr Palmer (a dice companion to the king, and possibly Cromwell). It was during this visit that a conversation supposedly took place between More and Rich in which they discussed the king's right to declare himself head of the Church, though this version of events is disputed.

It is worth noting that Rich and More had known each other for some time, most likely from when Rich was a teenager, and More acknowledged this in his trial. The two of them may not have been friends, but they were at least long-time acquaintances, with More already sensing in Rich's early days the type of man he would become: 'You were esteemed very light of your tongue, a great dicer, and of no commendable fame. And so, in your house at the Temple, where hath been your chief bringing up, were you likewise accompted.'[5] But did More envision Rich literally perjuring himself and turning ruthlessly against him? Most likely not, but he would probably not have been too surprised.

A conversation certainly took place between the two in the confines of the Tower and was an exchange back and forth on the power of parliament. More was no doubt happy to be engaged in such a discussion, to keep his mind occupied in the absence of his writing material, and he couldn't exactly ignore Rich in his cell. They both recounted different stories about that was discussed. More stated that the conversion was purely hypothetical and not a true account of his feelings. Rich, on the other hand, testified at the trial that More openly and categorically denied the king's authority as Supreme Head of the Church. Surely More would not have been so foolish as to state this openly. This is why most believe Rich bent the truth in order to provide evidence of More's guilt. Another version of events is that Cromwell, on receiving the report of the conversation, saw an opportunity to twist the truth to suit his own ends and thereby convict More. Rich, in his role as Solicitor-General, then played his part in convicting More.

In her biography of More, historian Joanne Paul believes that More did not exactly incriminate himself, and it was Cromwell, on reading Rich's report of the conversation, who saw what they could use to convict More:

> All three lawyers – More, Rich and Cromwell – knew that the putting of cases was theoretical, a legal game to stretch the juridically inclined mind. In such a context, More's statements could not fall under the "malicious" denial of the Treasons Act. But what if they were removed from the realm of the hypothetical? Or rather, what if they were presented to those who didn't understand the game? Cromwell had the ammunition he needed.[6]

Truth or lie, or just manipulation, it would be this conversation that would provide the 'evidence' needed at More's trial to secure his death sentence. The supposed interaction of More and Rich is described in the account of William Roper, son-in-law to More after marrying his daughter, Margaret, in 1521. After More's execution, Roper authored a written account of More's arrest, imprisonment and death in a book titled *The Life of Thomas More,* which was first published in 1626:

> Shortly hereupon Mr. Rich then newly the King's Solicitor, Sir Richard Southwell, and Mr. Palmer, servant to the Secretary, were sent to Sir Thomas More into the Tower, to fetch away his books from him [...] Mr. Rich, pretending friendly talk with him, among other things of a set course, as it seemed, said thus unto him:
>
>> "Forasmuch as it is well known (Mr. More) that you are a man both wise and well learned, as well in the laws of the Realm, as otherwise, I pray you therefore, Sir, let me be so bold as of good will to put unto you this case.

> Admit there was, Sir, an Act of Parliament, that all the Realm should take me for the King, would not you (Mr. More) take me for the King?" – "Yes, Sir," quoth Sir Thomas More, "that would I." –
>
> "I put the case further," (quoth Mr. Rich), "that there was an Act of Parliament that all the Realm should take me for the Pope, would then not you, Mr. More, take me for the Pope?" – "For answer," quoth Sir Thomas More, "to your first case, the Parliament may well (Mr. Rich) meddle with the state of temporal princes; but to make an answer to your second case, I will put you in this case. Suppose the Parliament would make a law, that God should not be God, would you then, Mr. Rich, say God were not God?" – "No, Sir," quoth he, "that would I not, since no Parliament may make any such law." – "No more" (said Sir Thomas More, as Mr. Rich reported him) "could the Parliament make the King supreme head of the Church." Upon whose only report was Sir Thomas More indicted of treason upon the Statute in which it was made treason to deny the King to be supreme head of the Church[7].

However, there is another document in the archives – quite damaged, but some parts are still legible – which historians believe to have possibly been Rich's account to Thomas Cromwell after the aforementioned conversation. It is worth comparing the two, because, though undated, this one was most likely written at the time, not from a letter that was then interpreted by a loved one and rewritten in a biography. Both documents could feasibly be the true version of events. (I am always one to believe there are three versions to an event, yours, mine, and the truth, which I think is quite suitable in this case).

Thought to have been written before the official indictment, this latter document starts by listing those present at the tower on the 12 of June, and then details the conversation between Rich and More, as follows:

> Richard Rich: "Ask you this case if it were enacted by Parliament that I should be King […] and who so ever says nay […]"
>
> Thomas More: "[…] put another hyer case whiche was this Sir I put case […] by Parliament that God were not God…"
>
> Richard Rich: "[…] hat act was not possible to be made to make God ungod but sir by cause your case is […] ye agree that ye were bound so to affirme & accept me to be Kyng.

> Thomas More: "The cases were not lyke by cause that a kyng [...] although the Kyng were accepted in England yet moste Utter parts do not affirme the same."
>
> Richard Rich then broke off the conversation and remarked on More's "concealment to the question" before wishing that "Jesus send you better grace." Then he left the cell taking with him all of More's books.

Rich's and More's conversation is interesting. They both use phrases such as 'put the case', or 'ask you about this case'. These phrases are from their days as trainee lawyers when debating a topic: 'The private feelings or conventions of the individual lawyer were in no way involved; it was highly theatrical and dramatic activity in other words calling for the wisdom and subtitle of the orator [...] it would be incapable more than anything he said should be taken to express his individual convictions.'[8] To More, conversing in this way would have seemed perfectly natural for two former law students. It seems, however, that Rich was being very cunning, using this method of debate to gain an insight into More's beliefs and to use it against him.

Not long after this visit, More faced a preliminary hearing, and on 26 June 1535 a special commission was established to hear his case. This was followed on the 28th by a 2000-word indictment accusing More of treason. The next step was a trial, although not as we know it today. In the sixteenth century, trials such as this one were merely a show. The verdict was already known, but the impression was given that the case had not already been decided. Trials such as this were used by the Crown to demonstrate its power, and to show the world of that the accused was guilty.

More's trial was held on 1 July at Westminster Hall and was presided over by 15 justices of the King's Bench, who had been chosen by the king. They included Thomas Cromwell, the Dukes of Norfolk and Suffolk, Thomas Boleyn, and his son, Viscount Rochford. All these men would be loyal to the king's cause (for their own benefit) and clearly knew what was expected. They were presided over by Audley, who was regarded as 'Chief legal authority [...] deploying his skills in treason trials, a field where he was generally regarded as an expert.'[9]

The Treason Act, which Henry VIII had passed in 1535, had defined the crime of high treason, as being committed by those who:

> do maliciously wish, will or desire by words or writing, or by craft imagine, invent, practise, or attempt any bodily harm to be done or committed to the king's most royal person, the queen's or the heirs apparent, or to deprive them of any of their dignity, title or name of their royal estates, or slanderously and maliciously publish and pronounce, by express writing or words, that the king should be heretic, schismatic, tyrant, infidel or usurper of the crown [...] their aiders, counsellors, consenters, and abettors, being thereof lawfully convicted according to the laws and customs of this realm, shall be adjudged traitors, and that every such offence in any the premises, that shall he committed or done after the said first day of February, shall be reputed, accepted, and adjudged high treason, and the offenders therein and their aiders, consenters, counsellors, and abettors, being lawfully convicted of any such offence as is aforesaid, shall have and suffer such pains of death and other penalties, as is limited and accustomed in cases of high treason.[10]

In simple terms, the act meant that anyone who refused the Act of Supremacy, like More and Fisher, were now considered to have committed treason against their king. The supposed conversation that More had with Rich was all the evidence the king needed to have the judges proclaim More guilty, for More had expressed *in words* that he thought the king to be a heretic.

More knew of the huge challenge he now faced, and most likely knew he was not going to survive the ordeal, but it did not stop him using all his legal knowledge to show his peers there was no legal case against him and that he was innocent. Reports describe More as being weak, so much so that he was allowed to be seated in a chair throughout.[11] 'He was bent, he wore the beard that a sick man wears, he was leaning on a cane like one of the unemployed beggars described in his utopia. More listened to the all-too-long indictment.[12] Although, in his own words, he could not remember all of the indictment, he nevertheless wanted to show the weakness of the case against him:

> "My lords, I do most humbly thank your honours of your great good will towards me. Howbeit, I make this my boon and petition unto God as heartily as I may, that he will vouchsafe this my good, honest and upright mind to nourish, maintain and uphold in me even to the last hour and extreme moment that ever I shall live. Concerning now the matters you charge and challenge me withal, the articles are so prolix and long that I fear, what for

my long imprisonment [...] that neither my wit, nor my memory, nor yet my voice, will serve to make so full, so effectual and sufficient answer as the weight and importance of these matters doth crave.

"Touching the first article, wherein is purposed that I, to utter and show my malice against the King and his late marriage [...] I never spoke anything against it, and that whatsoever I have spoken in that matter, I have none otherwise spoken but according to my very mind, opinion and conscience. In the which if I had not, for discharging of my conscience to God and my duty to my prince, done as I have done, I might well account myself a naughty, unfaithful and disloyal subject.

"The second Charge against me is, That I have violated the Act made in the last Parliament [...] I had never said nor done anything against it; neither can any one Word or Action of mine be alleged, or produced, to make me culpable. Nay, this I own was then my Answer to their Honours, that I would think of nothing else hereafter, but of the bitter Passions of our Blessed Saviour, and of my Exit out of this miserable World. I wish no body any harm, and if this does not keep me alive, I desire not to live; by all which I know, I would not transgress any Law, or become guilty of any treasonable Crime: for this Statute, nor no other Law in the World can punish any Man for his Silence.

The Attorney:

"Sir Thomas, tho we have not one Word or Deed of yours to object against you, yet we have your Silence, which is an evident sign of the Malice of your Heart: because no dutiful Subject, being lawfully ask'd this Question, will refuse to answer."

Sir Thomas More:

"Sir, my Silence is no sign of any Malice in my Heart [...] And as to what you say, that no good Subject will refuse to give a direct Answer; I did really think it to be the Duty of every good Subject, except he be such a Subject as will be a bad Christian, rather to obey God than Man; to be more cautious to offend his Conscience, than of any thing else in the whole World ; especially if his Conscience be not the Occasion of same Sedition and great Injury to his Prince and Country : for I do here sincerely protest, that I never revealed it to any Man alive.

"I come now to the third principal Article in my Indictment, by which I am accused of malicious Attempts, traitorous Endeavours, and perfidious Practices

> against that Statute, as the Words therein do allege, because I wrote, while in the Tower, divers Packets of Letters to Bishop Fisher; whereby I exhorted him to violate the same Law and encouraged him in the like Obstinacy. I do insist that these Letters, be produced and read in Court, by which I may be either acquitted or convinced of a Lye; but because you say the bishop burnt them all, I will here tell you the whole truth of the matter. Some of my Letters related only to our private Affairs, as about our old Friendship and Acquaintance: One of them was in answer to his, wherein he desired me to let him know what Answers I made upon my Examinations concerning the Oath of Supremacy; and what I wrote to him upon it was this, That I had already settled my Conscience, and let him satisfy his according to his own Mind. God is my Witness, and as I hope he will save my Soul, I gave him no other Answer; and this I presume is no Breach of the Laws.
>
> "As to the principal Crime objected against me, that I should say upon my Examination in the Tower, That this Law was like a two-edged Sword; for in consenting to it, I should endanger my Soul, and in rejecting it should lose my Life: To conclude, I do sincerely avouch, that I never spoke a Word against this Law so any Man living, tho perhaps the King's Majesty has been told the contrary.[13]

Rich was then called to give evidence of the conversation that had apparently taken place said between the two. Thomas More responded to this:

> If I were a Man, my Lords, that had no regard to my Oath, I had had no occasion to be here at this time, as is well known to everybody, as a Criminal; and if this Oath, Mr. Rich, which you have taken be true, then I pray I may never see God's Face, which, In good Faith, Mr. Rich, I am more concerned for your Perjury, than my own Danger; and I must tell you, that neither myself nor anybody else to my knowledge, ever took you to be a Man of such Reputation, that I or any other would have anything to do with you in a Matter of Importance. You know that I have been acquainted with your manner of Life and Conversation long time, even from your Youth to the present Juncture, for we lived in the same Parish; and you very well know, I am sorry I am forced to speak it, you always lay under the Odium of a very lying Tongue, of a great Gamester, and of no good Name and Character either there or in the Temple, where you was educated. Can it therefore seem likely to your Lordships, that I should in so weighty an Affair as this, act so unadvisedly, as to trust Mr. Rich, a Man I had always so mean an Opinion of, in reference to

> his Truth and Honesty, so very much before my Sovereign Lord the King, to whom I am so deeply indebted for his manifold Favours, or any of his noble and grave Counsellors, that I should only impart to Mr. Rich the Secrets of my Conscience in respect to the King's Supremacy, the particular Secrets, and only Point about which I have been so long pressed to explain myself? which I never did, nor never would reveal; when the Act was once made, either to the King himself, or any of his Privy-Counsellors, as is well known to your Honours, who have been sent upon no other account at several times by his Majesty to me in the Tower. I refer it to your Judgments, my Lords, whether this can seem credible to any of your Lordships.
>
> But supposing what Mr. Rich has sworn should be true, seeing the Words were spoken in familiar and private Conversation, and that there was nothing at all asserted, but only Cases put without any offensive Circumstances; it cannot in justice be said, that they were spoke maliciously, and where there is no Malice, there is no Offence. Besides, my Lords, I cannot think so many reverend Bishops, so many honourable Personages, and so many virtuous and learned Men, of whom the Parliament consisted in the enacting of that Law, ever meant to have any Man punished with Death, in whom no Malice could be found. Therefore this Word Maliciously is so far significant in this Statute, as the Word Forcible is in that of Forcible Entry; for in that Case is any enter peaceably and puts his Adversary out forcibly, it is no Offence, but is he enters forcibly; he shall be punished by that Statute.[14]

More then requested Southwell and Mr Palmer to be called, both of whom had accompanied Rich that day. However, they could neither confirm nor condone what Rich had said, responding that they were so busy collecting More's books that neither heard what was discussed. It seems they either genuinely did not hear what happened or did not wish to face the wrath of the king, Rich and Cromwell by defending More.

> Then answered the Duke of Norfolk: "We now plainly perceive that ye are maliciously bent." "Nay, nay," quoth Sir Thomas More, "very and pure necessity, for the discharge of my conscience, enforceth me to speak so much. Wherein I call and appeal to God, whose only sight pierceth into the very depth of man's heart, to be my witness."[15]

Not only had More and Rich worked alongside each other as colleagues, but it is most likely, as More stated himself, they had known each other a long time. More's defence against Rich's statement, and his strong religious views, are a clear indication that Rich had clearly interpreted the conversation to suit the king's needs and was not speaking the truth. But did the king or Cromwell ask Rich to do this or had he done it off his own back? Although the trial was merely for show, the jury still needed some evidence to confirm the charge of treason. They knew, as did More, that most of the charges against him were very flimsy. It would be Rich's testimony, and that alone, which enabled the jury to return after just 15 minutes with a verdict of guilty and for More's sentence to be pronounced, to no surprise to anyone including More himself.

More's silence could not be attributed as an act of high treason. He had used legal process as his defence and the judges had to accept this and dropped their charges against him, leaving Rich's testimony as the only evidence that could be used to condemn him. On hearing the verdict, More now took the opportunity to speak his mind. He wanted on record the injustice and absurdity of the trial, and to have a clear conscience when he went to the scaffold.

Audley, sitting as High Chancellor throughout the trial, has been criticised by historians for allowing Rich's testimony. He was a trained lawyer and knew More's arguments had merit and would be hard to answer. He turned to Lord Fitz James, Lord Chief Justice of the King's bench:

> and asked if the indictment was sufficient. The latter was a more learned lawyer than Audley and therefore more sensitive to the force of More's words. All he could say was "My Lordes all, by St. Julian I must needs confesse, that, if the Act of Parliament be lawful, then the Indictment is good enough."[16]

More's sentencing was an act of pure spite on the part of the king, carried out against someone he considered a friend, for not giving in and accepting him as supreme head. More had made Henry look stupid, and had also given others ideas to speak out. We will never know if the king had spoken privately to Rich, instructing him to do what he did. Or, knowing his master's wishes, did Cromwell use Rich's conversation and instruct Rich to twist it in order to frame More. Or had Rich taken it upon himself to purge his words in order to satisfy the king's wishes, not caring for his mortal soul like More? Looking at Rich's actions later in his life, it certainly would not have been out of character for him to have committed perjury in order to advance himself by giving the king what he clearly wanted – the removal of Thomas More. All three scenarios could certainly have been the truth.

* * *

So, what led to More's eventual execution? Henry VIII did not deal with betrayal well, especially from those whom he considered close and whom he held dear. More was his friend, someone he trusted and with whom he could chat to openly about politics and religion. When More refused to take the oath, Henry at first tried to give him space, allowing him to step away from court and politics. However, this actually made More more of a thorn in the king's side. As a private citizen he could speak more openly about his views, something that Henry began to see as dangerous. Henry became more and more disgruntled at his friend, and thoughts of betrayal began to set as More would not bow to the king's demands. Why should More refuse when most of the other nobles and men of the court were accepting? These thoughts would ultimately lead to Morse's arrest and confinement in the Tower, where Fisher was already being held due to his meetings with the Maid of Kent. Furthermore, by allowing More and Fisher not to take the oath, it could be seen as a precedent for others to pick and choose what they did and did not accept from their sovereign.[17] This went against Henry's belief as being anointed by God. Henry wanted More to be punished for his actions, and was manoeuvring behind the scenes to ensure that happened. Everyone involved in the case knew what the outcome had to be. Cromwell knew what the king wanted and even tried to get More to take the oath to save himself, but More would not budge, even though he knew it would lead to his death.

More certainly did not expect his words to be twisted by Rich and used against him. What brought Rich to seemingly perjure himself in such a way? We will never know for sure, but the obvious answer is clearly to enable the king to get what he wanted. If it had not been Rich, then something would have been done to have brought about More's supposed treason. There is no evidence that the king forced Rich's hand in giving evidence, but nothing should surprise us with Henry. That said, Rich most likely did what he did willingly, by having the conversation with More in the first place, and with the intention of getting him to slip on his words in order to bring his case to trial. Rich acted out of a desire to please the king.

Is there any likelihood of More actually saying what Rich claimed he had? Possibly. As a final note, Rich's role in More's execution is one of the most significant pieces of evidence produced to explain his greedy and villainous nature: that he perjured himself against More, who is thought of today as a saint, for personal gain. However, More was not the saint that he is believed to be today. It was because of his imprisonment in the Tower and eventual execution for his beliefs which led to his becoming a martyr and a saint. If he had not been executed, then he would most likely not be held in such high regard.

The Dissolution and the Court of Augmentations

Upon making himself head of the Church in England, after denying the Pope's authority, Henry set about closing the monasteries and claiming their wealth for the Crown, a series of processes known as the dissolution of the monasteries, which began in 1536 and can be considered as the triumph of the monarchy over the church.

That the king was able to do this was thanks to his resourceful, loyal and knowledgeable advisors, who were able to find ways to enact his will within the law; men such as Cromwell and Rich. Another reason why the break with Rome and the dissolution of the monasteries were allowed was the fact that many laymen in England envied the wealth of the church and were distrustful of the Pope.

It was around the same time that a new religion was gaining ground in Europe: Protestantism. This new religion, although still under the umbrella of Christianity, differed from Catholicism in many ways. It lay great store on the importance of private devotion, while minimising the organised, sacramental aspects of religious services. The focus was more on a one-to-one relationship with God, and the new churches eschewed elaborate decoration, relics and saints. Protestants also insisted that the Bible should be translated into English, and that religious services should be held in English so they were accessible for all. Above all, the new religion declared that the Pope had no authority, that the only authority coming from God was the Bible.

The new religion brought with it huge changes throughout Europe, and also in England, as more and more people began to follow and accept it, including Cromwell and Anne Boleyn. This was another reason why members of the court accepted Henry as the head of the Church and denounced the Pope. It added to the support of the dissolution, and Henry was well aware of its popularity. Although he did not agree with it fully, he used some of the Reformist ideas to break from Rome. And though still a Catholic at heart, he did not agree with being answerable to the Pope. After all, why should he have to share its wealth and power when he could have it all to himself. Those politicians who were not extremist in their views on religion, saw the break as a way to benefit morally. As for the bishops who followed the dissolution, they saw it as their duty. After all, their positions and wealth were given to them by Henry and they felt obliged to follow his rule. Furthermore, the king was placed there by God's will and so disobeying the king meant disobeying God himself.

The justification given by Henry and his ministers for the dissolution was to restore Christianity to what it was in the beginning and to purge it of any corruption that had been introduced by men along the way. A number of Henry's nobles, and members of the gentry, began to see there were financial gains to be had with the closing of the monasteries; i.e., they would be able to acquire more land and therefore wealth. No one, whatever their views on what the king was doing, wanted to miss out on their share of the spoils. At the start of 1536 letters began to appear in court from these men enquiring into how they could purchase the various monastic sites.

The First General Act was passed in March 1536:

> Forasmuch as manifest sin, vicious, carnal and abominable living is daily used and committed among the little and small abbeys, priories and other religious houses […] where the congregation of such religious persons is under the number of twelve persons, whereby the governors of such religious houses, and their convent, spoil, destroy, consume, and utterly waste, as well their churches, monasteries, priories, principal houses, farms, granges, lands tenements, and hereditaments, as the ornaments of their churches, and their goods and chattels, to the great infamy of the King's highness and the realm, if redress should not be had thereof […] and by a cursed custom so rooted and infested, that a great multitude of the religious persons in such small houses do rather choose to rove abroad in apostasy, than to conform themselves to the observation of good religion; so that without such small houses be utterly suppressed, and the religious persons therein committed to great and honourable monasteries of religion in this realm, where they may be compelled to live religiously for the reformation of their lives […]

> [...] shall be much more to the pleasure of Almighty God, and for the honour of this his realm, that the possessions of such religious houses, now being spent, spoiled, and wasted for increase and maintenance of sin, should be used and converted to better uses, and the unthrifty religious persons so spending the same, to be compelled to reform their lives.
>
> And it is also enacted, by [...] The king's highness shall have and enjoy to his own proper use, all the ornaments, jewels, goods, chattels, and debts, which pertain to any of the chief governors of the said monasteries.[1]

The act called for the closure of monasteries that earned less than £200 a year. Those nuns and monks of the 376 monasteries that were closed were either placed in a larger monastery or given a pension to live off. Some claim that the act was drafted by Audley and Richard Rich, rather than Cromwell who wanted a slower and gentler approach,[2] which is in in keeping with Cromwell's usual strategy. He always tried to please the masses whenever possible, preferring not to alienate anyone unless it could not be helped. This suggestion of the idea not being Cromwell's is also hinted at in a letter from the French ambassador in June 1540, which was written after the arrest of Cromwell:

> They have given him for colleague a new Chancellor of the Augmentations, the most wretched person in England, who was first inventor of the overthrow of abbeys, and of all innovations in the Church – in fact, he invented and Cromwell authorised – and he had the title of the Augmentations for having increased the King's revenue, but might be called, from another point of view, Chancellor of the Diminutions, for having diminished the wealth of the Church and his reputation as a learned and wise man.[3]

He was not the only person to state this view. Thomas Wyatt, a member of the Privy Council and Henry's court, would also write it in his papers in 1536:

> Whereupon the Lord Audelie then Lord Chancellor & the said Richard Ritche devised two Actes thone for the suppression of the monasteries not being above the valewe of 1001 yerelies & thother for the erectinge of this new Court wherin they placed onely their freindes & servants to be ministers. When this act was read in the parliament, all the abominations of theis religious persons, which was before in the visitacion fownd was opened which abhorred

> all mens ears to heare. And that such wickedness should [not] be known to the people, for doubt lest they should be therwith infected, it was thought better that it should be touched in thacte by generall wordes then declared in particularitie as it was done indeed.[4]

Those instructed to close the smaller monasteries, the Titles Commissioners, were instructed to:

> repair to the monasteries and take into their hands the common and convent seals and cause them to be broken or safely kept to the King's use [...] They shall call before them the governors and officers of the said houses, and make them declare upon oath the state and plight of the houses, and what leases, corrodies, fees, &c. have been granted by them before 4 Feb shall make a true inventory of the buildings (and stock such as late, corn etc) survey all the possessions, spiritual and temporal, inquire of the debts due to the houses, appoint pensions to the governors and notify them to the Chancellor and Council of the Court of Augmentation, with the total values of the possessions; then despatch the governor and other religious persons with convenient rewards [...] pay all servants' wages and debts due for corn, cattle, victuals, &c., and all other debts not exceeding 6l. 13s. 4d[5].

The dissolution of the monasteries was the biggest change of land ownership in English history, with around a sixth of the land changing hands. In order to manage such a huge operation, the Court of Augmentations was created, with Richard Rich being appointed its chancellor. He had the legal knowledge and administrative skills to manage such an operation, and the post was most likely created with him in mind. He worked with Audley to draft the Act establishing the Court. In this capacity, and in his role of Solicitor General, he became Cromwell's second in command in matters of the dissolution, the 'lesser hammer' as some would phrase it.

The Augmentations was modelled on the Duchy of Lancaster, which had been established in 1399 and is responsible for managing the land, property and finances of the County of Lancashire (including areas of Manchester and Merseyside today). This included land and holdings outside of the area but owned by the Duke of Lancaster, which were administered separately from Crown lands. The Augmentations took this idea but simplified it.

> Under the new arrangement all crown lands of the Court, irrespective of previous tenure, were included in the accounts for the county of their location. To equalize the administrative burden of receipt and audit, several counties of England and Wales were grouped together according to the extent of holdings in different areas of the country. Ministers' accounts, therefore, were not drawn up under the name of the monastery or family unit but by counties within the circuits, which, with the exception of Yorkshire, included two or more counties. so that land was assessed according to geography rather than ownership: 'Ministers' accounts were not drawn up under the name of the monastery or family unit but by counties within the circuits.[6]

The opening of the Act establishing the Court of Augmentations is as follows:

> maketh established and erecteth a Ctayne Courte commonly to be called the Courte of Thaugmentacions of the Revenues of the Kinges Crowne which Courte by auctoritie aforesaid contynually shalbe a Courte of Recorde and shall have one Greate Seale and one Privie Seale to be engraved and made after suche fourme fasshion and man as shalbe appoynted by the Kinges Highnes and shall remayne and be ordered as hereafter shalbe declared Also be it enacted by auctoritie aforesaid that there shalbe one atayne psone to be named and assigned by the Kinges Highnes which shalbe Chauncello of the said Courte and shalbe Chieffe and Principall officer of the same Court and shalbe called Chauncello of the Courte of Thaugmentacions of the Revenues of the Kinges Crowne and shall have the keping of the said Greate Seale and Privie Seale … Also that there shalbe one psone …which shalbe called the Kinges Treasourer of the Courte of Th augmentacions…there shalbe one psonne lerned in the Lawes of the Land to … be called the Kinges Attorney of the said Courte and shalbe the thirde officer … one psonne to be…the Kinges Solicitour of the said Courte and shalbe the fourth office…there shalbe tenne pticular Auditors … there shalbe xvij pticular Receyvours … one psonne to … called Clerke of the said Courte and one other psonne which shalbe Vussher of the same Courte and one other … called Messanger … edy of them shall have suche yerely fees rewardes … the office of Chauncellourshippe of the Augmentacions … shall ministre equall justice to Rich and pore to the best of your connyng witte and power and that ye shall diligently pcure all thinges which maye honestly and justly be to the Kinges advantage and pfitte and to the Augmentacion of the rightes and progatyves of his Crowne.'[7]

In simple terms, the Court would manage the confiscated wealth from the closure of the monasteries, including collecting and paying any debts, reviewing old leases, and creating new ones, arranging the sale or property and exchanges, processing pensions, and, most importantly, creating new revenues for the Crown. With no established base at the start, the Augmentations were based at Rich's townhouse in London, and at Leighs, in addition to using some space at Westminster Hall. Eventually, permanent offices were acquired within Westminster Palace, with a royal warrant being issued on 31 January 1537 to the Treasurer of the Augmentations to pay Anthony Denny, 'keeper of our manour besides Westminster and payemaister of our buyldinges there,' £662 1*d.* for the construction of a house 'for the Officers of our augmentations'.[8] The treasurer was Thomas Pope, a servant of Thomas Audley, who was paid £120 (£52,953.24 at today's value). He would be responsible for surveying the monasteries. An attorney was also appointed, John Onley, who received a fee of £40l (£17,651.08 at today's value) and there were solicitors,[9] with clerks and messengers to pass information from person to person.

The land was organised by counties, with one auditor appointed per county, 15 in total. Accompanying the auditor would be a surveyor and receiver, who would have other local ministers under their supervision. Their main purpose was to administer the lands now owned by the Crown following the dissolution, and soon the Augmentations became an important part of the machinery of the Tudor government.[10]

In order to retain some kind of income from the lands given to his nobles and gentry, the king had included in the act the following: 'any estate of inheritance there should be reserved to the king and his heirs a tenure by knight service, and an annual rent of one tenth of the current net annual value of the property concerned.'[11] This was most likely added after it was realised the king was losing out on future profit by selling most of the monastic land. Whether he came to this realisation himself (it was possible), or if it was someone else, we will never know for sure. It could also have been another way of nominal recognition of the Crown's trial superiority.[12]

As Chancellor for the Augmentation, Rich was usually in constant attendance at meetings of the Privy Council. Sometimes he would receive direct instructions in meetings, though the normal procedure would have been to transmit these by messenger.[13] In the records there were letters and notes, some from Rich to Cromwell and vice versa, which gives an indication into the various goings-on of the Augmentations, and how Cromwell was kept informed of what Rich was doing:

> *26 October 1532, Christopher Hales to Cromwell*
> Since my last, Mr. Rich and I are at a point with Roberts the auditor for his lands which were Mrs. Lubbyshed's near Copthall. Roberts and Rich behaved well, but the former would not part with the land except to the King. We have promised him 220l, which he gave for it. He says it is worth 400 marks. We long for the King's return.[14]

Some letters show Rich trying to direct people towards his preferred way (whether it was right for them or not), trying to come across as a friend and ally, especially to those who were close to the king, such as the Duke of Suffolk:

> *3rd Aug 1535, Rich to the Duke of Suffolk*
> I have, by the King's commands, received a letter from Mr. Secretary [Cromwell], which I beg you to consider and follow the King's pleasure. As one who is much interested in your welfare, I advise you to desire no recompense for the reversions, but to surrender them frankly.[15]

Others show Rich looking out for those he considered friends (or maybe just useful people to keep sweet):

> *4th July 1536, Rich to the Abbot and Convent of Evesham*
> The Lord Chancellor and Lord Privy Seal have written to them in favour of Rich's friend John Fletewood, gentleman, servant to the Lord Chancellor, for a lease of the farm of Penortham. Requires them to let his friend have it at once, since no more of their convent shall have the same. At the Friar Austens in London.[16]

There is even evidence of the king monitoring the transactions of the Augmentations and giving his own instructions, which Rich was most certain to make sure were followed through:

> *12th Aug 1536, Henry VIII to Rich*
> Notwithstanding the King's recent resolution for the continuance of certain monasteries, and among others that of Stanfeld, Lincoln, yet finding much inconvenience would ensue by its preservation, the Commissioners are now instructed to suppress it entirely, and Rich is to make a lease of the site and demesne lands to Robert Tyrwitt, one of the esquires of the Body, and arrange with him for the purchase of the stock and moveable goods. For the reception of the religious who shall be put out of Stanfeld, Rich is to take a fine of 900 marks of the monastery of Stixwold, Lincoln…reserving to the King's use lands to the value of 34l. 10s. 7d. a year only, and according to the former determination put out all the religious there resident and let those of Stanfeld take their places, letting the monastery of Stixwold stand after this translation. Monastery of Chersee[17].

Rich for the most part would always try to stay within the confines of the law, even if he did manipulate it. If there was an opportunity to enrich himself then he would, always making sure to cover his tracks if it was something he knew others would frown upon:

> *15th August 1536, Rich to Cromwell*
> Remember Cold Park and the manor of the same. Do not let it be known it is for me; and obtain the King's pleasure, for his Grace said he would have it himself. Since writing hereof, I have received your other letter about lady Guldeford. I shall do my best. I will certify your lordship by Saturday or Sunday concerning Clementhorppe. I will, for your sake, send for the books with expedition.[18]

He knew the importance of not alienating his colleagues in the court.

In April 1537 there is a letter from Sir Brian Hastings to Cromwell, trying to persuade him to do all in his power to keep the nearby nunnery of Hampole open. He writes to Cromwell instead of Rich as it seems 'the Chancellor of the Augmentations will not suffer it to pass the seal, for what cause I know not'.[19] By writing to Cromwell, who was of a higher authority than Rich, Hastings may have hoped Cromwell would override Rich, which was within his power to do.

* * *

Rich and his assistants did not shy away from their work and meticulously assessed every building and assets, and although the surveys would usually be done by local officials of the court, at times, in special circumstances or when the council had requested immediate surveys, Rich and other members of the council would assist.[20] The surveys were usually carried out to determine boundaries and measurements of a site or to ascertain the value of the pieces of land.[21] In one instance Rich and Pope, along with Richard Pollard (of the Court of Surveys) and Richard Southwell (receiver for Augmentations), spent three weeks in Essex, Suffolk and Norfolk. It was a time he did a lot of travelling across the country. In a letter to Henry and his council, Rich detailed the surrender of the monastery of Bury, Suffolk:

> *7th November 1539, Rich, and others, to Henry VIII*
> [...] have, on Tuesday after All Saints, taken the surrender of the monastery of Bury and made an inventory. Have not as yet assigned the late abbot any pension, but suggest that, as he has been very conformable and is aged and the yearly revenues of the house will be 4,000 marks, he should have 500 marks a year and a house. Have taken into their own custody, for the King, the plate and best ornaments of the house and sold the rest; they were not of such value as might have been expected. The lead and bells (if the house be defaced) will be worth 4,500 marks. Beg to know whether to deface the church or other edifices of the house and will meanwhile survey the lands. Have set one awork to make a true "platt" of the house, which they will bring with them. Late monastery of Bury, 7 Nov. Signed by Sir Richard Rich, Sir Antony Wyngfeld, Ric. Southwell, William Petre, John ap Rice, and Thomas Myldemaye[22].

Although managed by Rich, who was answerable to the king, Thomas Cromwell, in his role as vicegerent in spirituals (second in command to the king in church matters), kept a close eye on the comings and goings of the Augmentations (evidence which has already been illustrated above). He would be the one recommending people like Rich for the specific roles, in fact all those appointed to the Court of Augmentations would be Cromwell supporters or dependent on him in some way. Although appointed by Cromwell, and they were, it seems, supportive of one another, Cromwell did not entirely leave the running of Augmentations to Rich,[23] who was not happy with being micromanaged. Records show Cromwell keeping in touch with the commanders who were suppressing the monasteries rather than waiting for information from Rich directly, and of men writing to Cromwell rather than Rich asking for his assistance in matters which came under the jurisdiction of Augmentations.

> *2nd June 1536, Sir William Goryng to Cromwell*
> I beg that Master Chancellor of the Augmentation may be so informed that the Commissioners be not troubled in viewing my priory, as it is not touched in the statute, as I have been seised of it two years at Michaelmas, with all the lands. I will send you the writings for your approval…[24]

Even men of high standing such as Arundel, who worked in Augmentations, knew that the real power lay with Cromwell and not Rich:

> *January 1537, Arundell to Cromwell*
> Riding downward to Cornwall and passing the monastery of Clyffe, hearing such lamentation for the dissolution thereof and a bruit in the country that the King at your lordship's suit had pardoned it, I sent to Mr. Chancellor of the Augmentations to know whether to dissolve it, as I had his letters for the dissolution of the residue of Somersetshire, and it seemed to be omitted by oversight, he being very busy. I beg in behalf of the honest gentlemen of that quarter that the house may stand. In it are 17 priests of honest life who keep great hospitality. The house would have stood if we surveyors had not found it of greater value than it was set at the first survey; but that was not the abbot's fault, for when the collector came for the tenth the abbot said he ought to pay more, and paid according to the later survey. The house will give the King 1,000 mks. for their exemption.[25]

Rich, already having a reputation as being corrupt and greedy, had alienated members of the court, most likely due to his involvement with More's downfall. As Chancellor in Augmentations, his greed seemed to grow or at least be more visible to others around him. In these letters, we start to gain a glimpse as to what his contemporaries thought of him, and he does not come across well. There was a dispute with the Priory of Fristock. John Husee (sometimes spelt Hussey) and the Lisles[26] were not happy with what Rich was doing and stated their dislike for him:

10 August 1536, John Husee to Lady Lisle
I have had much to do with the Chancellor of Augmentations since my coming. I find small friendship in him; yet he has appointed my lord 86l. a year out of the priory of Frystock, so that, the 100l. reserved, my lord must become tenant to the King for the rest. I have caused two bills to be made, the one for a gift to my lord, your ladyship, and the heirs of your bodies; the other with remainder to the heirs of my lord's body. I fear he will speed but the first, for he is full of dissimulation. He would in nowise put Mr. Basset in the remainder, though I promised him a velvet gown. I doubt he will deserve neither thanks nor reward. "He passeth all that ever I sued unto."I have followed Mr. Hennage for the 1,000 marks. He gives fair words, but small comfort. He refers all to my lord Privy Seal; so it will be no short suit. I can see no remedy, but, as my lord's pleasure is, to go thorough with Hide, where Mr. Windsor and I will do our best for my lord's advantage.[27]

6th September 1536 John Huseey to Lord Lisle
Never found anyone like the Chancellor of the Augmentations. He paid no heed to your letter, and he says that the King will have all the lead of the suppressed abbeys brought to London and refined. Fristok and the lands are let to George Carewe for 21 years, so unless you compound with him you shall have only the bare rent after your patent is out. Details other vexatious objections made by the Chancellor. Does not trust his promises. I fear he will get your patent for life only. Will be in hand with my lord Chancellor for the two denizens when he comes to town. Has been in hand with Mr. Vice-Treasurer "concerning this money"; but I cannot get from him 100 marks, as his friends cannot help him. But if provision could be made for the 400l., he will make shift for the 24l. Fears that Botton and Hide are confederate with lord Beauchamp.[28]

6 September 1536, John Husee to Lady Lisle
The Chancellor of the Augmentations is not the man you take him for. He says he will procure to have the remainder to my lord's heirs, but I do not trust him. Still, he shall lack no calling on while I am at Court. You will see by my lord's letter how he has handled me. I have been with Mr. Vice-treasurer, as desired by my lord and you; but he says he has tried all his friends, and none will help. I did not advise my lord to sell the land the King gave to him and you, but rather to make some shift with it than lose the other… I hope the matter will be paid or respited. I will ride to the Court at Grafton tomorrow about it.[29]

23 December 1536, Richard Lee to Lord Lisle
The Chancellor of the Court of Augmentations sticks at lord Lisle's suit for the priory of Fristock, but John Husee and Lee will speak to lord Privy Seal about it, and doubt not that lord Lisle will obtain the fee simple, as he wishes.[30]

1 September 1537, John Husee to Lord Lisle
As to your patent, I cannot get the Chancellor of the Augmentations to set his hand to the book, but I doubt not to pass it without him or his hand. He has constrained me to search the Parliament roll for the danger of it, for I would be loath to stand in his courtesy. As far as I could see, he never meant your lordship good, but I trust to make it sure in spite of his teeth. I think it grieves him that you have the fee simple without his help.[31]

18 September 1537, Rich to Lord Lisle
Before I knew of the King's grant of the priory and parsonage of Frythelstock to your lordship and lady Lisle, I had promised the lease of the parsonage at lord Beauchamp's request to one Walter Farr. I beg you to grant it now to him at the rent as it was valued to the King. At the beginning of next term you shall have your letters patent sealed. The Augustyne Friers in London.[32]

16 October 1537, John Husee to Lord Lisle
The chancellor of that court is not your friend and what has been done was "maugre his head". Hopes to bring Lisle's patent[…][33]

Reading both the words of Lisle and Husee is a little window onto others in the court who most likely felt the same towards Rich. He did favours for people and sent instructions, but they knew he only did so if there was something in it for him. They were distrustful of him, but did they have genuine cause, or had they already made up their minds, and whatever Rich did would never be seen with good intentions?

* * *

It seems that those in the court and members of the Tudor gentry and nobility were already suspicious of the members of the new Court of Augmentations, and of their real intent. It is worth noting the majority of those assigned to Augmentations, though ambitious, were men who relied on their own ability, not men born into privilege. So, of course they would do their utmost to please the king and Cromwell. They may also have seen the opportunity to enrich themselves, legally, while doing their job, and this has led to them being branded as greedy and unscrupulous.[34] Some men, like Rich, may have abused their position a little too much, and as they already had a reputation for being dishonest it was inevitable that rumours and accusations would start to circulate within court.

As officials of the Augmentations, they were resented locally because they represented influence and power. Moreover, they had the authority of the Crown behind them, which made those around them envious. People like Sackville, Rich, Edward North, Thomas Pope, and the Mildmays – Walter and Thomas – all established family fortunes from the profits of monastic acquisitions; but so did the Greshams – John, Richard, and Thomas – William Paulet, Ralph Sadler, Thomas Wriothesley, Charles Brandon, Edmund Peckham, and countless other enterprising individuals who were shrewd enough to make the most of an advantageous market. It was a vigorous, expanding age, and most ministers active in public life were in one way or another carried along on the current of national prosperity.[35]

For most, the accusations were merely a result of jealousy, or perhaps misunderstanding of their roles. For those like Rich, who were certainly greedy, the accusations of dishonesty may have been true, but he was acting within the the law so that no one could call him to account. The king would have heard the rumours, but, for a time, as long as Rich was bringing in more money, he was happy to turn a blind eye to any potential corruption.[36]

The time came, however, when Rich had to defend himself against accusations and potential charges. The first time he was accused and faced charges was on 7 April 1541. The accuser was John Hillary of Keynsham Abbey in Somerset, who accused Rich of withholding information concerning the deception of the late abbot of Keynsham, as a result of which the Crown suffered a loss of 200 marks. Rich had to stand before the Privy Council to hear the charges and must have been worried, knowing full well that others might distort the truth. Fortunately for him it was decided that John Hillary had 'slanderously and untruely forged the said mattier,' and instead of Rich facing punishment, Hillary was himself placed in Marshalsea prison.[37]

Even the king himself had charged Rich of embezzlement – twice. However, the charges were dropped before a final hearing was heard, due to lack of evidence. It is worth noting here that monarchs knew that their servants helped themselves to certain bonuses, and that this was one of the perks of the job. It was when those bonuses were taken from the Crown's own pocket that action was taken. We can be fairly certain that if there was a shred of evidence against Rich then Henry would not have let it drop. Whatever had been flagged to the king seems to have come to nothing.

Many years later, under Mary I, these accusations of corruption arose once more: that Rich had profited from the sale of lead, had appropriated for himself manors sold by the king to another, had deliberately misrepresented the value of certain lands alienated by the Crown, and, on numerous occasions, had effected exchanges of property without taking indentures or sureties for payment.[38] However, as previously, no actual evidence could be produced, so Rich did not face any penalties. And though today cannot make any definite judgement, it does make one wonder that maybe there was truth in the allegations but that Rich was too intelligent and knew the right people to get away with his crimes.

In his book, *The History of the Court of Augmentations*, Walter C. Richardson goes on to say that we should not judge Rich by the standards of today but by the standards of the sixteenth century. He most certainly did profit from his position in the Augmentations, and like most officials of the time, he accepted gifts[39] and backhanders, though without the guilt that many of those around him felt. But Rich's reputation was also besmirched by other shady dealings, not least of which was his role in Thomas More's downfall

* * *

In his capacity as Chancellor of the Court of Augmentations Rich was able to expand his land portfolio and establish himself as one of the great landowners of the time,[40] which only fuelled his reputation as a greedy villain. He was, in effect, able to choose what land he wanted, and, to a certain extent, to control who was allowed to buy land from the king in other areas, including Essex, land surrounding the Leighs estate, and land that was granted through the dissolution. Henry even granted Rich the land of Syon Abbey around Felsted in 1537, which enabled him to further expand his estate.[41]

All grants of land are not listed here, but a few examples are given below:

25 May 1537

Agnes the abbess and the convent of the Augustinian monastery of St. Saviour and SS. Mary and Bride, Syon, Midd. Licence to alienate the following possessions to Sir Ric. Rich, …and dame Elizabeth his wife…A field called Southfeld, a meadow called Gale mede, adjoining the said field with land in Felsted, Essex, parcel of the manor of Felsted, which Ric. Vowell, for merly prior of the priory of St. John the Evangelist, Lighez, Essex, …2 crofts, called Bubland, in Felsted…another called Bubland, … another called Lovescrofte, and another called Holdewynescrofte, in Felsted…3 crofts, with a grove adjoining in Felsted, near Badys Lane …2 acres of wood in Felsted…3 crofts of land in Felsted…100 acres of land…called Cabells and Prestyes, in Felsted…a tenement and 60 acres of arable land…a field, called Rode Feld, another called Freets, a wood called Graunt Courts parke, a meadow called Levynges mede, parcel of the manor of Graunt Courts, in Felsted.[42]

5 March 1538

Sir Ric.Rich…and Elizabeth his wife. Grant in fee of the reversion of the lands and rent reserved upon a lease by Thomas, the prior, and the convent of the suppressed monastery of St. Mary, Pritwell, Essex…[43]

26 April 1539

Licence to alienate the manor of Fyfylde…and certain lands…in Fyfild, Norton, Morton, Shelley, Parva Laver, Willingale Doo and Willingale Spayne, Essex, and the advowson of Fyfild church, the manor of Herons in Fyfyld… the manor of Ladihall alias Overhall in Morto…and certain messuages, lands, &c. in Morton, Fyfyld…High Laver, Parva Laver and Bobyagworth…and also a portion of lands and wood in Fyfhide which the abbot and convent of Waitham Holy Cross, by powers conferred upon them by Act of Parliament… alienated to the said Richard…Robt. Noke, clk., John Chauncy, and Rich Lynsell, to the use of the said Richard Rich and his heirs for eve…to Walt. Pharr, and John Haver to the use of the said Richard Rich, and Elizabeth his wife, and the heirs, male…[44,45]

29 May 1540
Sir Ricard Rich...To be bailiff of the lordship or manor of Northwelde, and keeper or parker of the park there; with fees of 20s. a year as bailiff, and 60s. a year as parker.

26 May 1542
Grant, in fee, of...the manor of Gladfen alias Gladfen Hall, and...the rectory of Matching, which belonged to the suppressed priory of Leghes, Essex, with all possessions of the priory in Halsted and Matching, Essex; and...the manor of Fawcet alias Fawcett Forest, Westmld, which belonged to the dissolved abbey of Bylande, Yorkshire, with Fawcett Wood and all other possessions of the abbey there and in Bannandesdale, Bannandesdalehed, Borowdale, Borowdalehed and Capullfall within the parishes of Kendal and Shapp, Westmld...[46]

4 June 1542
Lease of the manor of Skrynes in the parish of Roxwell, and lordship of Wretell, Essex, and a close called Long Lee formerly in tenure of Thos. Sampford, which premises came to the King by the attainder of Ric. Fermor; with reservations; for 21 years.[47]

2 July 1543
To be keeper of the manor and park of Wanstede, Essex, and bailiff of the manor of Wanstede; with 2d. a day as keeper and 26s. 8d. a year as bailiff.[48]

15 February 1546
Grant, in fee for the manor of Parva Badowe, Essex, and...the lordships and manors of Myddelton alias Mylton, Southchurch, Lawling and Stysted. Essex, and all other lands in those places which formerly belonged to Christchurch cathedral, Canterbury.[49]

Rich would leave his post as Chancellor of the Court of Augmentations in 1544, with Edward North taking over the position after an initial crossover period of the two. There would be little variation of the court for the first ten years of its creation. However, as the land started to be sold and changed hands there was less and less work for the Court. It was finally dissolved on 23 January 1554.

* * *

The year 1536 was one of significance to Henry VIII, and of a number of events changed the course of English history. One of these was the execution of Anne Boleyn. She and Cromwell had managed to work alongside one another due to similar interests, but though they were both of Reformist beliefs, they did not want the same things. Cromwell's main goal was to serve his king, who saw the dissolution as an opportunity to enrich the Crown. Anne, although wanting to break away from the papacy, did not agree with the monasteries' wealth going into the royal coffers, believing it should be going to charity instead.[50] This disagreement would eventually lead to the realisation that one of them had to go. Anne, thinking she was in the stronger position, even threatened to have Cromwell's head. Cromwell, however, was not unduly concerned. He felt secure in his role and knew the king was growing tired of her. He is said to have told Chapuys, the Spanish ambassador, 'I trust so much on my master, that I fancy she cannot do me any harm.'[51]

Cromwell knew that he would need allies against Anne and began to reach out to the Catholic faction, men and women completely opposed to his own views and plans. He sent Rich in July 1535 to warn the Duke of Suffolk of the king's displeasure at the 'decay' of certain houses that the duke claimed to have restored, as well as a number of other gripes. He knew they wanted rid of her as much as he was beginning too, and instructed Rich:

> to say somewhat to the saide Duke in this matier alledging unto him that as I am, alwayes haue been, and euer wilbe his graces poure frende so I requere him not to stycke with [i.e. object to] the kinges highnes in this matier…I pray you shew him on my behalf that my poure and frendelie aduise is that his grace shall liberally wryte to the kinges highnes in this matier so as his highnes may thereby perceyue the saide Dukes gentill herte and naturall zele towardes his maieste aswell in this as in all other thinges.[52]

Rich, as Solicitor General, would have been involved in Anne's downfall and eventual execution. Knowing it was what the king and Cromwell both wanted probably made it easier for him to follow through on his duties, and perhaps he even felt it compensated for his wrongdoings to More (inasmuch as Anne was a reformer and Rich was a catholic).

* * *

Due to his close proximity to the king, Rich was able to build a trust with Henry, thus enabling him to gain more power and influence. This was not something for which Rich can be blamed as many of those in positions close to the king would do the same. To gain patronage of the monarch himself was the goal of the majority of the men who entered court life, men such as Cromwell, Audley, Edward Seymour and Anne Boleyn's father, Thomas.

The accusation that Rich was greedy and profited from the dissolution can be levelled at others, though he was in a better position than most to get what he wanted. Along with Rich, some of those who profited from the dissolution include Brown, Paget, Paulet, Russel, Edward Seymour and Wriosthesley. These men were members of the new administrative elite who owed their positions at least in part to the king,[53] but more importantly, they were men who supplied much of the political weight and the administrative talent to maintain the Tudor government.

For Rich the dissolution and the creation of the Court of Augmentations really pushed him into the limelight and allowed him to shine. Although he and Cromwell may not have entirely trusted each other, they each knew their worth and were cut from the same cloth – hardworking, intelligent and loyal servants to their king. As Chancellor of Augmentations Rich was able to build his mini kingdom in Essex, allowing him to enrich himself and become one of the main players in the Tudor court. He was not worried if he did not make friends; his focus was on people knowing who he was and the power he wielded. The events of the mid-1530s were significant in the course of English history and one cannot ignore the involvement of Rich.

The Downfall of Thomas Cromwell

Richard Rich's story cannot continue until there is a brief overview of one man who, in addition to Thomas More, would have a huge impact on Rich's life. That man is Thomas Cromwell, with whom Rich is associated from the dissolution in 1536 until Cromwell's execution on 28 July 1540 – which Rich played a part in. How much influence did Cromwell have over Rich and how much of an impact did he have on the latter's career. Did Rich turn against the man who had taken him under his wing, or was he once more carrying out the king's wishes?

Thomas Cromwell was born around 1485, most likely in Putney, London. He came from a working-class family (his father, Walter, owned a hostelry). He had a very different upbringing than those who would be his colleagues in Henry's court, even referring to himself being a ruffian in his earlier years (his father had been arrested for watering down his beer, and, on another occasion, was convicted of assault).

Today, many remember him as being the man behind the Dissolution of the Monasteries, and by some historians, like Elton, as being responsible for modernising the Tudor government. He was certainly intelligent enough to rise in the ranks of Henry's court, holding positions such as chief minister to the king from 1532 to 1540, Vicegerent of spirituals/Vicar General in 1535–1540, and Lord Chamberlain 1540, all titles he held until his arrest and execution.

Before entering the Tudor court, Cromwell spent some time in Europe as a mercenary, most likely in France, before heading to Italy where he was employed in the household of a wealthy Florentine merchant called Francesco Frescobaldi. While there, Cromwell experienced a different culture to that in England, and even France, and it is thought this had an impact on his beliefs and views. On returning to England, he decided to follow a profession in the law. He also married Elizabeth Wykes, a widower, whose father had served King Henry VII. It seems to have been a happy marriage, and they had three children – Alice, Grace and Gregory – who all resided in the City of London. Tragedy struck the family in the years 1528–9, when his wife and both daughters died of the sweating sickness, leaving him his only son, Gregory. Cromwell never remarried.

Securing the patronage of Wolsey, Cromwell entered the life of the Tudor Court and was quick to learn the ways to survive. He seemed to be a man most people got on with: even the Spanish ambassador, Eustace Chapuys, who would be on the opposite side to Cromwell in the divorce of Catherine of Aragon and the break with Rome, had kind words to say about him.

> *21 November 1535, Chapuys to Antoine Perrenot de Granvelle, minister to King Phillip II of Spain:*
> The secretary, Cromwell, is the son of a poor farrier…Cromwell was ill behaved when young, and after an imprisonment was forced to leave the country. He went to Flanders, Rome, and elsewhere in Italy. When he returned, he married the daughter of a shearman and served in his house; he then became a solicitor. The cardinal of York, seeing his vigilance and diligence, his ability and promptitude, both in evil and good, took him into his service…At the Cardinal's fall no one behaved better to him than Cromwell. After the Cardinal's death Wallop[1] attacked him with insults and threats, and for protection he procured an audience of the King, and promised to make him the Richest king that ever was in England. The King immediately retained him on his Council but told no one for four months. Now he stands above everyone but the Lady, and every one considers he has more credit with his master than Wolsey had…He speaks well in his own language, and tolerably in Latin, French, and Italian; is hospitable, liberal both with his property and with gracious words, magnificent in his household and in building…[2]

Cromwell, like others, had witnessed Wolsey's rise to power, but unlike most, he was pleased for him rather than envious of someone who, like himself, was from 'low stock'. He witnessed how far a man like him could rise, if he put in the hard work. Wolsey supported and rewarded his friends, and those loyal to him, and soon Cromwell found himself on the council, and a close confidant and friend of Wolsey.

When Wolsey fell from favour in 1529, Cromwell stood by his friend and tried to support him as much as he could, even when those around him turned away from the ex-Lord Chancellor. Cromwell even approached the king to petition a pardon for Wolsey. It was refused, but the king was impressed by Cromwell's loyalty, a trait he valued in his own ministers.

Cromwell's behaviour during Wolsey's downfall also displayed other characteristics that were useful in a Tudor politician – an attitude of irreverence, and an ability in the law.

Cromwell's humble beginnings, in sharp contrast to many of the ministers and nobles in Henry's court, gave him an education in life and survival, and it was these skills that enabled him to climb his way up in society while making himself useful to the king. When it was clear that no more could be done for his former employer and friend, Cromwell began to look to improve his own career by giving the king the one thing he wanted most, and which Wolsey had failed to: an annulment. He knew that if he was successful it would place him high on the king's list of favourites.

Cromwell's first formal office was Master of the Jewels,[3] to which he was appointed in April 1532. It was around 1530 that he caught the attention of Anne Boleyn, who was also rapidly rising in the court. The two aligned with one another thanks to their common enthusiasm for reformation, but they were not exactly friends. As soon as the tide – and Henry – started to turn against her, Cromwell began to set in motion events that would lead to her death on the scaffold. He knew there was a chance it could be her life or his own on the line because they had both risen so high in the king's circle. He aligned himself with the Seymours, a new rising family, one of whom, Jane, had now caught the king's eye.

Cromwell was a professional who was able to separate business from pleasure. He served Henry like a loyal dog, and those who prevented him from enacting the king's wishes, whether considered friend of foe by Cromwell, found themself duly dispatched. He was an agent of the royal will[4] and would always try to use parliamentary statute to achieve this. Those who followed him, like Rich, were able to watch and learn. Historian Tracey Borman describes Cromwell as having a

> brilliant mind and capacity for hard work […] shrewd […] driven by a desire to succeed in all things […] ready wit, brilliant cover, irreverent and warmth[…] when […] engaged in a conversation that interested him […] his face

> would like up and take on a range of expression[5][...] he enjoyed art, literature and music, [was a] keen gardener [...] and [had] a love of falconry ...[an]... affable and generous host [...] a person of good cheer, gracious in words and generous in actions.[6]

His personality and behaviour gained him respect, to a point, by those loyal to his cause and those on the opposite side, like Chapuys. Cromwell was an approachable man who was happy to give favours to those who asked. He was able to befriend those in the ruling and middle classes alike.[7] He kept his ears open at all times and even listened to gossip should it be useful at some point[8] further down the line.

* * *

By 1536 Cromwell had already begun to make enemies, both within the court (due to his closeness to the king and his common background), and with Catholics, especially those in the north. This is most likely due to his role in the dissolution. Those who were still of the Catholic faith blamed Cromwell for the break with Rome, and rather than attack the king, they attempted to have Cromwell his allies removed from power.

The rebellion, known as the Pilgrimage of Grace, was started in Yorkshire in October 1536, and was a result of the numerous changes Henry VIII and Cromwell had brought about, including the Dissolution of the Monasteries. There were two separate uprisings: the first was in Lincolnshire, and the second, which was the larger and more significant of the two, was in Yorkshire, and headed by a man named Robert Aske. Those who led the uprisings demanded that Henry return to the old Catholic ways and restore Princess Mary back into the line of succession. In order to not offend the king, they protested against those advising him, most notably 'that heretic' Cromwell, rather than against Henry himself. It is estimated that around 50,000 people in the north, from all walks of life including members of the nobility and knights, joined the revolt and took the 'Pilgrims Oath':

> Ye shall not enter to this our pilgrimage of Grace for the common wealth, but only for the maintenance of God's Faith and Church militant, preservation

> of the King's person and issue, and purifying the nobility of all villains' blood and evil counsellors; to the restitution of Christ's Church and suppression of heretics' opinions, by the holy contents of this book.[9]

In mid-October 1536 the Duke of Norfolk was appointed by the king to confront the rebels. He arranged to meet with the leaders, including Aske, at Doncaster on 26 October. They met again in December, when a truce had been agreed, and the rebels presented their demands (known as the Pontefract Articles). There were 24 demands in total, nine of which were religious, including an end to all further closures of monasteries and a return to papal authority. The other demands were economic, legal and political and included a demand that all the rebels be pardoned, that a parliament be held in York, and there be an end to enclosures. The articles also included a demand for the surrender of Cromwell, Richard Rich, and the heretic bishops who were 'up to no good', and that they be banished and punished as 'subverters of the good laws of the realm and maintainers and inventors of heretics'.[10]

Genuinely believing the king would agree to their demands, the rebels promised to end the uprising and return to their homes. Clearly they did not understand their king, who loathed being told what to do. When the news of the uprising reached the court, Henry had his nobles and gentry raise men from their estates to be sent north to help disband the rebels. This was common practice, and Rich was one those who raised men from his estate to help.[11]

The king had no intention of giving into their demands: he knew it, his nobility knew it, and so too did the rebels when there was no sign of their demands being met. The rebels decided to attack Scarborough Castle, and other sites, to show Henry they were serious. This played right into his hands, however. The attack was just the excuse that Henry needed to go back on his promise. He had the leaders rounded up and punished. Some 216 of them were executed, including Aske who was hanged at York on 12 July.

* * *

Although Cromwell, Rich and Cranmer stayed in their positions after the Pilgrimage of Grace, things had begun to change, especially for Cromwell.

It seemed the king was beginning to keep Cromwell at a distance, starting a pattern of blaming others for his own choices. The king was even violent towards his minister on at least one occasion in 1538, when a courtier described how Henry pommelled Cromwell about the head 'as if he were a dog'.

Cromwell, meanwhile, thought he had found his chance, not only to get back in the king's good graces but also to bring England closer to the Reformist countries (with whom he himself identified) by finding the king a new wife. Jane Seymour, who Henry had married on 30 May 1536, tragically died from complications a week after giving birth to Prince Edward, on 24 October 1537. The king was distraught at the loss, but knew he needed to remarry, and so Cromwell set about looking for a new bride. Rich did not play a direct part in the search.

Eventually, a bride was found, Anne of Cleves, from western Germany. When Anne arrived in Calais on 11 December 1539, she was met by numerous English dignitaries, including Rich, John Dudley, Thomas Dennys and Thomas Arundell.[12] All those present were dressed in 'coats of satin damask and velvet, besides the said lords, who wore three collars of cloth of gold and purple velvet and chains of gold, and 200 yeomen… in the King's colours, red and blue cloth.' On entering Calais, two English ships in the dock nearby, decked in gold and silk banners, let off 200 shots as she passed,[13] in a salute to the future queen. She then sailed for England and arrived on 27 December 1539.

Anyone who is familiar with Henry VIII and his six wives will know the outcome of the union, with Henry declaring to Cromwell 'I like her not!' and demanding an immediate end to the marriage, a task not so easily achievable. Anne, who was intelligent enough to understand Cromwell's standing, had even written to him, desperate for assistance in keeping the king happy. Cromwell, though, knew how angry Henry would be if he spoke up for Anne, and decided against it, reporting her letters to the king. Cromwell realised the mess he was in. He was not able to give the king what he wanted, leaving him on dangerous ground.

Although Anne tried to please the king by adapting her dress and trying to learn English, it was not enough. Henry had already made up his mind and wanted rid of her, and Cromwell would be held accountable. Despite this, on 18 April 1540, Henry appointed Cromwell as Earl of Essex, a title of high standing for one of such humble beginnings, and also made him Lord Great Chamberlain.

Cromwell may have breathed a sigh of relief after this, hoping that he had managed to weather the storm, but it was soon clear that all was not forgiven, and the king was merely playing games with him. Henry started questioning Cromwell about the religious disputes going on in London, nothing new but something he had not shown an interest in previously. He was looking for a way to get rid of his minister. Maybe Cromwell's enemies had placed the idea in the king's head, we do not know, but Henry's mind was made up. The unrest in London was due to the dissolution. Henry would have remembered how the people were unhappy with Dudley and Empson at the end of his father's reign, and how he had used them as scapegoats. And so he decided to allow the blame for the widespread anger at the Dissolution to be placed at Cromwell's door. Henry had begun to realise that Cromwell was becoming more of a nuisance than a useful minister.

On either 6 or 7 June, there is a record of Cromwell and Wriothesley conversing. Cromwell asked if there was any news on the marriage and divorce, and Wriothesley replied there was none. Wriothesley asked if Cromwell had any work for him, to which he replied, 'No, I have no business now, but one thing is stuck in my head, which troubles me, and I thought to tell you. The king said he does not like the Queen, he has not liked her from the beginning. I believe she is still as much of a maid as she was when she came to England.'[14] Wriothesley exclaimed, 'For God's sake…devise relief for the king, or we shall both smart for it.'[15]

Cromwell's enemies, led by the Duke of Norfolk, knew it was best to strike while he was out of favour with the king. They were aware of the possibility of Cromwell getting back into the king's good graces, and this seemed more likely after he was made Earl of Essex. A whispering campaign was started against Cromwell, and of his supposed plot to bring about the king's downfall, something that everyone close to Henry knew he would not ignore. These whisperings of Cromwell's supposed betrayal spread far. In the Spanish chronicle (written by an unknown author) it tells us that Norfolk told him:

> It appears to us that Cromwell's intentions are not good […] None of us, however high we may be in the State, have so many servants as he has, and I can prove that in all parts of the kingdom people are wearing his livery and calling themselves his servants, under shelter of which they are committing a thousand offences.[16]

Norfolk went on to say to the king:

> May it please your Majesty, none of us, however high we may be in the State, have so many servants as he has, and I can prove that in all parts of the kingdom people are wearing his livery and calling themselves his servants, under shelter of which they are committing a thousand offences.

While the Marquis of Exeter warned, 'I know that he has arms in his house for more than seven thousand men, and we do not like the look of it.' Some of the nobles even went as far as to hint that Cromwell had the intention of making himself king, which Henry replied, 'My lords, I beseech you to put up with it for the present, and I promise you I will find a way to take his power away from him.'[17] The knife was twisted further for Cromwell when an unnamed gentleman, who had dined with Cromwell and Chapuys, claimed that Cromwell had said aloud that he hoped to be king one day. This unnamed man reported this to Norfolk and Seymour who were quick to report to the king, who responded, 'I may inform you that I greatly suspect him of a design to raise the kingdom and murder me.'[18]

The king was playing his usual game of making men and breaking them simultaneously if they offended him. He allowed Cromwell to continue, and even raised him higher in anointing him Earl of Essex, even though behind the scenes he was beginning to plot his downfall. Although Cromwell managed to get an annulment for Henry, it was clear that he had failed his king, a man who was used to getting his own way, and to make matters worse, the king had also been made to look a fool. Cromwell knew this. So too did those around him, including his enemies, and those whom he considered allies such as Rich.

On 10 June 1540, while leaving parliament to go to dinner, Cromwell's hat was blown off in a gust of wind. What made him aware that something was awry was that no one went and picked it up for him, which was considered a sign of respect. Cromwell, on collecting it himself noted, 'A high wind indeed must it have been to blow my bonnet off and *k*eep all yours on,' to which he was ignored, and everyone around him continued to go to dinner.[19] While they dined, Cromwell was ignored, another strange occurrence, and after dinner Cromwell and others entered the chamber where they were all seated. Sensing something was afoot, Cromwell spoke once more, 'You were in a great hurry, gentlemen, to get seated.'

He was then called traitor by those around him, many with anger and hatred in their voices. His friends, such as his nephew, Audley, and Cranmer were present, and although they did not join in the aggression, they did not defend him either. Another man present was Richard Rich, who was experienced enough to know how to play the game. Cromwell was arrested by Kingston, and throwing his cap on the floor, he exclaimed:

> I am no traitor! Your Grace, members of the Council, is this reward for good service done unto His Majesty the king? I put it to your consciences, am I a traitor as your accusations imply? Well, no matter, for I renounce all pardons or grace needed, for I never offended the king, and it matters only if the king himself thinks me a traitor, and he would never have me linger long!

Norfolk pulled Cromwell's golden collar from his shoulders, while Fitzwilliam pulled the garter from his leg.[20] He was then taken to the tower, where he had sent so many before him, and was lodged in the queen's rooms.[21]

The following is an account from the French ambassador of Cromwell's arrest and the events of the following day.

> *23 June 1540, Marillac to Montmorency (a French noble and constable):*
> As soon as the Captain of the Guard declared his charge to make him prisoner, Cromwell in a rage cast his bonnet on the ground, saying to the duke of Norfolk and others of the Privy Council assembled there that this was the reward of his services, and that he appealed to their consciences as to whether he was a traitor; but since he was treated thus he renounced all pardon, as he had never thought to have offended, and only asked the King not to make him languish long. Thereupon some said he was a traitor, others that he should be judged according to the laws he had made, which were so sanguinary that

> often words spoken inadvertently with good intention had constituted high treason [...] Next day were found several letters he wrote to or received from the Lutheran lords of Germany. Cannot learn what they contained except that this King was thereby so exasperated against him that he would no longer hear him spoken of, but rather desired to abolish all memory of him as the greatest wretch ever born in England. To commence, this King distributed all his offices and proclaimed that none should call him lord Privy Seal or by any other title of estate, but only Thomas Cromwell.[22]

Had Rich known which way the wind was blowing, and did he then go to the king? Or did the king ask Rich to acquire the evidence to secure Cromwell's execution? By August of that year, he was a member of the Privy Council.[23] Was this his reward for services rendered?

* * *

It has already been noted that Cromwell's crime was failing the king by not giving him what he wanted. Rich, always in the background, knew this has been a big mistake, and on seeing the way the consensus was going with Cromwell, soon jumped on the bandwagon. It may also have been due to his religious values which also allowed him to turn against a man who had, it seemed, been an esteemed colleague. Cromwell, was of the Reformist persuasion, whereas Rich only assisted in the dissolution for financial gain, not because he was against the Pope.

> It remains to name those who have succeeded to Cromwell's estates [...] For affairs of justice they have deputed the Chancellor, who, among other virtues, can neither speak French nor Latin, and has the reputation of being a good seller of justice whenever he can find a buyer. They have given him for colleague...[the]...chancellor of the Augmentations, the most wretched person in England.[24]

In a letter to the King of France on 10 June, Marillac, the French ambassador, explained the events of Cromwell's arrest and how after the king had contacted him to explain the reason for his arrest:

> … the innovations in religion of which Cromwell was principal author. The substance was that the King, wishing by all possible means to lead back religion to the way of truth, Cromwell, as attached to the German Lutherans, had always favoured the doctors who preached such erroneous opinions and hindered those who preached the contrary, and that recently, warned by some of his principal servants to reflect that he was working against the intention of the King and of the Acts of Parliament, he had betrayed himself and said he hoped to suppress the old preachers and have only the new, adding that the affair would soon be brought to such a pass that the King with all his power could not prevent it.[25]

The king had made up his mind and decided that Cromwell was a traitor. Unlike More, Cromwell did not have the chance to speak in his defence in a trial. More had presented his case very well, and those on the jury knew in their hearts that he was most likely innocent of his charges against him. They knew that Cromwell was also innocent and that he was a more experienced lawyer than More. So, in order to prevent him defending himself they persuaded the king (although he was probably happy to agree, knowing what the outcome would be) to pass a bill of attainder against Cromwell. It was Rich who would produce a lot of the information required[26] to draft this bill of attainder. Once more he had turned against those who had helped promote him. Was he just going with the tide in order to save himself rather than out of malicious intent? Most likely.

The only one who spoke up for Cromwell was Cranmer, but he did not want to face the wrath of the king, and as he had done with Anne Boleyn, he accepted the accusations against Cromwell. In his letters to the king three elements are present; warm praise of the accused, horror of what he had been accused of, and also concern for the king at the loss of a brilliant advisor.[27] Cranmer knew how to stay on the king's right side while keeping his conscience clear.

> I heard yesterday in your Grace's Council that he is a traitor, yet who cannot be sorrowful and amazed that he should be a traitor against your Majesty, he that was so advanced by your Majesty; he whose surety was only by your Majesty; he who loved your Majesty, as I ever thought, no less than God; he who studied always to set forwards whatsoever was your Majesty's will and

> pleasure; he that cared for no man's displeasure to serve your Majesty; he that was such a servant in my judgment, in wisdom, diligence, faithfulness, and experience, as no prince in this realm ever had; he that was so vigilant to preserve your Majesty from all treasons. I loved him as my friend, for so I took him to be; but I chiefly loved him for the love which I thought I saw him bear ever towards your Grace. But now, if he be a traitor, I am sorry that ever I loved him or trusted him, and I am very glad that his treason is discovered… but yet again I am very sorrowful; for who shall your Grace trust hereafter, if you might not trust him?[28]

Knowing his chances of survival were now minimal, Cromwell knew his only hope was speaking directly to the king. There was no way would Henry visit Cromwell at the Tower, or allow him to visit, so Cromwell wrote a series of letters, pleading his imminence and asking the king to let him live, and even reminding the king that sharks like Rich had no morals. In one of those letters, dated 12 June 1540, Cromwell wrote:

> Most gracious King and most merciful sovereign, your most humble most obedient and most bounden subject and most lamentable servant and prisoner, prostrates at the feet of your most excellent majesty. I have been accused to your Majesty of treason, to that I say I never in all my life thought willingly to do that thing that might or should displease your Majesty and much less to do or say that thing which of itself is so high and abominable offence, as God knows who I doubt not shall reveal the truth to your Highness. My accusers your Grace knows God forgive them. For as I ever have had love to your honour, person life, prosperity, health, wealth, joy, and comfort, and also your most dear and most entirely beloved son, the Prince his Grace […] God so help me in this my adversity and confound me if ever I thought the contrary. What labours, pains and travails I have taken according to my most bounden duty, God also knows, for if it were in my power as it is God's to make your Majesty to live ever young and prosperous, God knows I would, if it had been or were in my power to make you so rich, as you might enrich all men […] You are more like a dear father, your Majesty, not offended then a master. Such has been your most grave and godly counsels towards me at sundry times in that I have offended I ask your mercy. Most gracious sovereign lord, to my remembrance I never spoke with the Chancellor of the Augmentations and Throgmorton together at one time. But if I did, I am sure I spoke never of any such matter and your Grace knows what manner

> of man Throgmorton has ever been towards your Grace and your preceding. And what Master Chancellor has been towards me, God and he best knows I will never accuse him. What I have been towards him, your Majesty, right well knows I would to Christ I had obeyed your often most gracious, grave counsels and advertisements, then it had not been with me as now it is. Sir, I have meddled in so many matters under your Highness that I am not able to answer them all, but one thing I am well assured of that, wittingly and willingly, I have not had will to offend your Highness, but hard as it is for me or any other meddling as I have done to live under your Grace and your laws, but we must daily offend and where I have offended, I most humbly ask mercy and pardon at your gracious will and pleasure. I most lowly aske mercy and pardon of your Highness. Sir, there was also laid unto my charge at my examination that I had retained, contrary to your laws. Sir, what exposition may be made upon retainers I know not, but this will I say, if ever I retained any man but such only as were my household servants but against my will God confound me, but, most gracious sovereign, I have been so called on and sought by them that said they were my friend that constrained thereunto. Sir, I do acknowledge myself to have been a most miserable and wretched sinner and that I have not towards God and your Highness behaved myself as I ought and should have done. I appeal to your Highness for mercy, grace and pardon in such ways as shall be your pleasure beseeching the almighty maker and redeemer of this world.
>
> Written with the quaking hand and most sorrowful heart of your most sorrowful subject and most humble servant and prisoner, this Saturday at your Tower of London.
>
> *THOMAS CRUMWELL*[29]

Cromwell's downfall came not only as a result of not keeping the king happy, but also because his enemies persuaded Henry that Cromwell was no longer trustworthy. Rich's betrayal probably would not come as a surprise to Cromwell. Maybe he never fully trusted Rich and their initial relationship never developed further. For a time their goals aligned, but as was the way of the court, as soon as the balance of power changed so too did Rich's loyalties. They also differed in their way of working. Unlike Rich, Cromwell knew the importance of trying to appease others and make allies, even if for a short time, while Rich was no strategist. And though he may not have initiated Cromwell's downfall, he certainly did not argue against it.

The king was not persuaded by Cromwell's pleas and an Act of Attainder was passed, condemning Cromwell to death without a trial (the irony being that he had made such a thing possible in 1537 with the execution of Margaret Pole). Cromwell was beheaded on Tower Hill on 28 July 1540. It was a horrific sight, with three blows of the axe needed to remove his head. His corpse was placed in the Chapel of St Peter ad Vincula.

Once again Rich had been involved in the downfall of someone close to him, though there were not many who were close to the king who did not have a part to play. Those whom Cromwell thought of as his friends risked exposing themselves if they spoke up for him. Knowing the king wanted Cromwell gone, why would they risk defending him? On this occasion Cromwell was seen by Catholics as a heretic. Rich himself was a Catholic at heart, so was he doing what he thought was right despite Cromwell aiding his career?

* * *

It is worth discussing at this point the role the King played in the downfall of More and Cromwell, and whether or not Rich's involvement altered the outcome. The king, although at times distant from the general day-to-day running of the court, knew what was happening in his country. He knew what his ministers were doing, and if he did not like it, he would have put a stop to it. He allowed his ministers to do most of the hard work for him, but if he felt they were not following his requests, lawful or not, he saw it as a betrayal and that was fatal for the minister involved.

We see a pattern with how Henry dealt with ministers who were no longer considered useful. They were made scapegoats for everything that went wrong in the country. The king was never to blame. Even those in the Pilgrimage of Grace knew well enough not to lay the blame at the king's door, even though many of them knew it was his responsibility. And once anyone was deemed to have betrayed the king, they would most likely find themselves in the Tower. As Charles de Marillac remarked, innocence was no safeguard against being charged with treason, for with an instrument of destruction so loosely phrased as the Act of 1534, any man could be accused 'of maliciously wishing, willing or desiring, by word or writing, the King's death; it all depended on the construction given to the words.'[30]

Those like More and Cromwell had no hope of getting any forgiveness. They had risen too high for the king to merely forgive and banish for a short time. Cromwell tried to save himself by seeking the king's forgiveness as directly as possible. More tried not to speak out against the king and chose silence, but this was used against him: 'though we should have no word or deed to charge upon you, yet we have your silence, and that is a sign of your evil intention and a sure proof of malice.' Many had fallen after the king turned against them: Thomas Cromwell, Richard Empson and Edmund Dudley died as scapegoats; Sir Thomas More for not agreeing with the king; the Earl of Surrey[31] and the Duke of Buckingham because their titles and dignity encroached too closely upon that of the Crown; Anne Boleyn for being too outspoken and not giving the king a male heir. None of these were actually guilty of treason; they were guilt of falling out of favour, or more precisely, of Henry turning against them. Given this fact, can anyone be viewed as malicious and evil for not speaking up in their defence, knowing they could face the same fate?

If Cromwell was not guilty of treason, why did he declare his guilt on the scaffold? The king, as the head of the country, is the one to whom they owed their allegiance, aside from God. As the later Stuart monarchs believed, the king was in effect God's anointed, so to go against him was to go against God, and under God's law, a subject's duty was to obey their king. To that end, they were guilty and accepted their fate.

> The law stood above personal ideas about guilt or innocence, and no matter how innocent the individual may have considered himself, once the law had passed sentence and found him guilty, then the victim was regarded by all, even by himself, as being worthy to die. As George Boleyn said, since he had been condemned by the law to die, he would no longer maintain his innocence but confess that he deserved death.[32]

Henry came to regret Cromwell's execution, and just weeks after his death he was mourning the loss of the most faithful servant he ever had. Months later he even turned on his ministers and accused them of bringing false charges against Cromwell,[33] which was true, though Henry could have saved Cromwell if he had wanted to. Some of his ministers wanted Cromwell gone, others like Rich were doing what their monarch wanted. Henry had lost his most exceptional servant, who was the mastermind of reforms in every aspect of England's religious, political and social life, and who himself said 'that there was nothing he desired so much in this world as to leave a good name behind him'.[34]

* * *

As for Anne of Cleves, her fate was also sealed, though she did not lose her life. She had enough sense to agree to what the king wanted, thereby preventing Henry from turning against her. A few weeks before Cromwell was executed, on 7 July 1540, the leading clergy of England met at Westminster and declared the marriage null and void. Anne was informed the following day by a group of men appointed by the king, including Rich, who informed her that she was no longer his wife and queen and would now be referred to as the king's sister. Her brother's ambassador, Karl Hust, reported that on hearing the news she cried and was heartbroken. It seemed she was clinging to the hope that the king would accept her. Once the shock had receded, she was probably able to take stock of her situation and feel fortunate to have not faced banishment and imprisonment like Catherine of Aragon, or execution like Anne Boleyn. She was instructed by the commissioners to write to the king, accepting her fate, which she did, signing it 'Your Majesty's most humble sister and servant.'[35] The king responded with kind words, offering to adopt her as his sister, and giving her precedence over all the ladies at court who were not his (future) queen or his daughters, and granting her an annual income as well as some residences for her to call home, complete with furnishings and staff.

* * *

When Anne Boleyn was arrested in 1536 – in which Rich played a part of in an official capacity as Solicitor General – a number of other members of the nobility were also arrested and most were executed. One man who was not executed was Thomas Wyatt. He was arrested and questioned, but his friendship with Cromwell saved him. In 1541 he was arrested once more for treason, not for supposedly having a relationship with the queen but because it was believed he had made disrespectful references about Henry to the ambassador of Spain. Although the precise details are not clear, it is worth noting that this may have been an attempt to get rid of him, as he was an ally of Cromwell. Once more we find Rich involved in this event, and it is interesting to note that Wyatt was placed under great pressure to confess, which he did,[36] only to recant it later, stating that his initial confession was forced from him. It is not clear if Rich was present for the questioning and evidence gathering, but we do know in later events that he was prepared to use torture to get results. *Wyatt* survived this second accusation and was released at the request of the king's new queen, Catherine Howard, whom the king had married on the same day as Cromwell's execution. Her mother was a family friend of the Wyatts so she may have reached out to Catherine to speak to the king. The new queen's request was granted, on condition that he take back his wife, from whom he had been estranged for 15 years.

* * *

The following year Rich was involved in the questioning of a servant of Richard Pate,[37] Bishop of Worcester and Henry VIII's ambassador to Spain, and someone who was quite vocal against the king's break with Rome. This caused some embarrassment for the English monarch, which, as we know, did not bode well. Pate decided to leave the country, which was why Henry requested that Rich and others question Pate's servant in his absence.

> One of the English ambassadors with him had mounted his horse and departed by night, and it is not known where he has gone. It is said that, secretly, he was always a good Christian, maintaining our religion, and that, finding himself out of England and at liberty, he is gone to live elsewhere out of his King's power.[38]

Henry would have an act of attainder passed against Pate in 1542, which deprived him of his bishopric. He only returned to England on the accession of Queen Mary, when he was re-appointed bishop of Worcester.

* * *

By 1541 Rich had befriended some of the most influential people in the court, including the king himself. He may not have been much liked, but he did his job, and he did it well. By now it was clear that, unlike Cromwell, Rich did not value friendships. There is no record of him speaking up for his former boss and colleague, and his involvement in numerous events from the early 1530s to 1541 clearly shows he was not one to shy away from betrayal. By 1540 Rich was a father to at least 12 children by Elizabeth. The family mainly resided in Leighs in Essex. Some of his daughters were already married and those who were not most likely being found a husband by Rich who was forging links and loyalties to continue his influence, especially in Essex and the neighbouring counties. The future looked promising for Rich, and his career was to rise even further. Cromwell's downfall had been another example for Rich of how to survive in the Tudor court. Cromwell had risen to great heights, but the higher one rose, the harder one could fall. Cromwell knew his job involved making many enemies who would turn on him as soon as they got the chance, even though he was doing the king's work. But Cromwell need not have got so close to the king and welded so much influence that he was in danger from his enemies. Rich learned that he could serve his king without getting too close.

After Cromwell: Factions and Torture

During the latter years of his reign, following Cromwell's death, Henry ruled differently. No longer did he allow one minister to gain as much power and authority as Wolsey and Cromwell had been allowed to acquire. There were still ministers who held power, position and wealth, though, and men such as Hertford, Lord St John, Wriothesley, Gardener, Browne, Wingfield and Paget would be the familiar names on the Privy Council until Henry's death.

In the summer of 1541, Henry VIII's fifth queen, Catherine Howard, whom he had married on 28 July 1540, just after Cromwell's death, was facing execution herself. She had been charged with treason for having a premarital contract before her marriage to the king, and for sleeping with another man while queen. Her arrest was brought about by Cranmer. He knew that telling the king face to face would place him in harm's way, and so he explained in a letter what Catherine's infidelities were and let the letter for the king to find at Hampton Court Palace.

Once more we find Rich's name in the arrest of a high-ranking member of the king's court. Rich would be one of the men charged with questioning Francis Dereham, one of the men accused of having been intimate with the queen. On 1 December 1544, the Privy Council wrote to Wriothesley: 'Send interrogatories, devised for the lady Dowager of Norfolk, for the King's approval. Meanwhile have appointed Mr. Comptroller, Mr. Chancellor of the Augmentations [Rich], and Mr. Solicitor to examine Derham, Damport, and Bulmer.'[1]

Dereham knew Catherine when she was 14 years old and in the household of the Dowager Duchess (her step-grandmother). Dereham was the dowager's secretary, and he and Catherine became sexually involved with one another. It would come out that the two referred to each other at this time as husband and wife, and may have even entered into some form of betrothal. Dereham then left the household to go to Ireland, and when he returned Catherine was queen. Dereham initiated contact with the new young queen, who would have been afraid of what he might reveal. He may also have hinted at having a place in the royal court, something that Catherine would not have wanted. The Howards most likely knew what had occurred between their daughter and Dereham, and would have wished to keep him close, especially due to his temper and his penchant for a public scene, though not too close to Catherine as to risk those in court questioning their relationship.[2]

Dereham was brought to the attention of Cranmer and the court by William Damport, a friend of Dereham's and someone who had been a member of the Dowager Duchess' household. Damport had revealed all under pain of torture, including the claim that Dereham had told him he wanted to marry the queen, and that once the king 'were dead I am sure I might marry her'.[3] Under the Treason Act of 1534, such talk of a monarch's death was illegal.[4] Not only would Henry be infuriated by Dereham having had sexual relations with his wife, albeit before he married her, he now had the excuse he needed to punish him.

It is likely Dereham could have been submitted to torture,[5] but it is interesting to note that despite this, and knowing he was under threat of execution, he would not admit to having said he had hoped for the king's death, or planning it, or sleeping with Catherine while she was queen.[6] Most likely Rich would have been present at the interrogations. Rich would also be involved in the questioning of Joan Bulmer, a lady in waiting for Catherine, who happened to be in the household of the Dowager Duchess at the same time as Catherine and Dereham. She would not had been submitted to physical torture, but she may have been subject to intense questioning[7] in order to get the information required from her.

Rich's involvement did not end there. He also had in his custody William Ashby, a servant in the dowager duchess' household. His testimony revealed that the duchess, on realising what was happening, had all of Dereham's notes and letters taken away and destroyed.[8] Another who was questioned by the Privy Council, of which Rich was a member, was the Countess of Bridgewater (sister to the 3rd Duke of Norfolk, who was also a Howard.

The dowager was brought in for questioning and confined to the Tower of London. While questioned she denied having any knowledge of Catherine and Dereham being intimately involved. When confronted with evidence that she had opened the coffers to destroy any written evidence, she exclaimed that she does this in order to avoid any evidence being destroyed. However, the council already had the testimony of Ashby who had told them he had witnessed the dowager searching Dereham's coffers and removing all the papers, which she then read through herself to check for anything incriminating. Ashby went on to say that she had seemed frantic, most likely because she knew that what they had been accused of was true and that she may have been guilty of allowing it to happen. The duchess knew what the king was likely to do, and felt that neither the queen nor Dereham should be executed for their affair as it had happened before Catherine became queen.[9] She also commented, 'but I am sorry for the King, for he taketh the matter very heavily'.[10]

No stone was left unturned in investigating Catherine's infidelities, and Rich was one of those involved. Initially, it was not clear if the king initially wanted rid of Catherine, but once the truth about her past affair with Dereham became known, we can be sure that Rich would have made sure the king's wishes were followed to the letter.

On 1 December Dereham was put on trial, along with Culpeper, who had entered an adulterous affair with Catherine while she was queen. A special commission was set up to arrange the formalities. This included Rich, as well as Audley, the Duke of Norfolk, and Wriothesley.[11] Rich's name was also be on the death warrant of both men, signed on 9 December.

Both men were sentenced to death as traitors and faced being hanged, drawn and quartered. Culpeper's sentence was reduced to a simple drawing and beheading,[12] rather than the horrific process of having his entrails pulled out while still alive. This was most likely because he had been a member of the court. Dereham, however, would face the full horrifying punishment for his involvement with Catherine.

> And the tenth day of December…Culpeper and Dereham were drawn from the Tower of London to Tyburn, and there Culpeper, after exhortation made to the people to pray for him, he standing on the ground by the gallows, kneeled down and had his head stricken off; and then Durham was hanged, membered, bowelled, headed, and quartered. Culpeper's body is buried at St. Sepulchres Church by Newgate; their heads set on London Bridge.[13]

Those who had been questioned for their involvement with 'hiding' the affair were placed on trial for misprision of treason.[14] They included Catherine's uncle, William Howard, his wife, Katherine Tilney, Joan Bulmer, Anne Howard, Robert Damport, William Ashby and others. One person who was not present at the trial was the dowager duchess, possibly because of her age. The trial was held on 22 December and once more a special commission was created with Rich, Audley, Wriothesley and others being involved.[15] They all confessed to the crime of misprision of treason and their punishment was 'perpetual prison, and to lose their goods, and the profit of their lands during their lives'.[16] Not all ended up being punished; some were later pardoned by the king.

Lastly, it was the turn of Catherine herself to be tried, along with her chief lady in waiting, Jane Boleyn, widowed wife of George, brother to Anne Boleyn. Catherine confessed to the charges placed against her and was sentenced to death on 21 January:

> for leading an abominable, base, carnal, voluptuous, and vicious life, like a common harlot, with divers persons, as with Francis Dereham...That she led the King by word and gesture to love her and (he believing her to be pure and chaste and free from other matrimonial yoke) arrogantly coupled herself with him in marriage and Also the said Queen, not satisfied with her vicious life...falsely and traitorously held illicit meeting and conference to incite the... [Thomas]...Culpeper to have carnal intercourse with her; and insinuated to him that she loved him above the King and all others. Similarly, the said Culpeper incited the Queen. And the better and more secretly to pursue their carnal life they retained Jane lady Rochford...as a go-between to contrive meetings in the Queen's stole chamber and other suspect.[17]

They were executed on Tower Green, in the grounds of the Tower of London, on 13 February 1542. Catherine was executed first, followed by Jane.

* * *

On 12 July 1543 at Hampton Court Palace, Henry VIII was married, for the sixth and final time, to Katheryn Parr. Twice widowed herself, Katheryn was from a family who had served Henry well. She seemed to be the opposite of his last wife, with no skeletons in her closet and a reputation of being kind to everyone she met. She came to the attention of the king while serving in the household of his daughter, Mary Tudor. The two were good friends and soon the king was smitten and declared his intentions. He was not looking for another marriage of physical activity and lust but more of a companion in his final years. Katheryn had eyes for Thomas Seymour, brother to Jane, but convinced herself it was God's wish she married Henry and so put her desire for Thomas aside.

All this time Rich was still working as Chancellor for Augmentations, arranging for surveys and the closures of monasteries and nunneries around England, with the full encouragement from the king:

> Henry VIII […] authorising Sir William Paulett, Lord Saint John, Sir Thomas Wriothesley, Lord Wriothesley, Sir Ricard Rich and Sir Ricard Southwell to sell Crown lands, lead, prizes taken from enemies […] with the assistance of the King's attorney and solicitor-general and the attorneys and solicitors of the Court of Augmentations, Duchy of Lancaster, and Courts of Wards and Liveries and of First Fruits and Tenths, and the clerk of the Court of Augmentations […] The Commissioners are not to meddle with any exchange or mere gift, or gift and sale mixed, or gift and exchange mixed, or exchange and sale mixed, concerning possessions within the survey of the Augmentations, nor with any mere gift or gift and sale mixed concerning possessions within the survey of the General Surveyors; which are to be bargained for by the chancellor and council of the Augmentations and by the General Surveyors.[18]

As the years went by there was less and less land to sort, and it seems that Rich had either grown tired of his role. So, when circumstances began to change, he was more than happy to relinquish his role in Augmentations.

By 1543 the king was well aware that he was getting old. He had tried to reclaim some of his youth by marrying Catherine Howard, but that had not turned out well and so he looked elsewhere for a much-needed ego boost. The opportunity came up when he decided to join Spain in their war with France. In May of that year England began its third cross-channel invasion of France, this time in an attempt to capture Boulogne.

War meant the need for men and supplies, and word went out from the king to his nobility and gentry to raise funds and forces. Rich was among those requested to raise men, both as Chancellor of Augmentations and as a landowner. In August 1542 he wrote to one of his tenants:

> The King commands me to levy 100 archers, 100 billmen, and 20 horsemen, as well within mine office of the Augmentations, as within mine own lands; and, considering that you are one of the King's farmers within the same, this is to pray and command you to provide a good gelding or horse with an able archer for the war, harnessed, to serve in my said number, to be ready at one hour's warning. London, (blank) of August.[19]

For Rich war also meant a new position, High Treasurer for the English army while in France, appointed by the king himself, on 1 May 1544. In order to do this, he had surrendered his office in the Augmentations, a post he had held for eight years. The new Chancellor was Edward North, previously the treasurer. Once again, it seems that Rich was selected specifically for the post, as the king wanted someone reliable and experienced in finances to oversee the French campaign. For the five months he was in France, Rich would be responsible for wages, supplies and transport[20]. He was to 'take allowance for conveyance of treasure to the under-treasurers… [to arrange] for provisions and other necessaries against France and Scotland and for charges of garrisons and fortifications in Ireland, Calais, Guinness, Hampnes, and of navies upon the seas.'[21] Under him were six clerks and a messenger.[22]

Before mobilising to France, Rich would work alongside Sir Thomas Wriothesley in assigning the financial resources required for the war. However, the costs he and Wriothesley had planned for went completely out the window, causing issues for both Rich and his counterparts back in England. Not all the accounts survive, but a memorandum of his outgoings from 1 May to 18 October 1544 record it as £424,692, a figure greatly in excess of his own and Wriothesley's forecast of the previous spring.[23] Rich would find it difficult to get the funds from the treasury to pay the troops, and it seems there were arguments on both sides of the channel about how much money was needed. The king himself tasked Norfolk and Russel to investigate where the funds had gone to make sure all was in order: 'at this present, Sir Richard Rich, high treasurer of the Wars, with 20,000l. for the army there, has commissioned him to learn how the treasure hitherto sent has been employed, and to take the names, retinues and entertainment allowed to each captain, and be certified of all charges, ordinary and extraordinary.'[24]

By September, when the siege of Boulogne was underway, Rich sought more funds from Wriothesley, explaining that the money sent previously would not cover what was needed. He wrote on 6 September:

> Has received his letter, and also, by Mr. Higham, 30,000l.; at the receipt of which he had not 1.500l. and this 30,000l. will scarce satisfy next pay day, 8 Sept. Begs him to accelerate the next mass of money sent, which must be here before 22 Sept. This night at 10 o'clock 30 of the Frenchmen issued out at a breach by the castle to win the bray which we had won, and there was a good skirmish and 9 or 10 Frenchmen slain. One Frenchman offered 300 cr. for his life but he suffered also. If powder come, we shall make the assault the latter end of this week and the town must be the King's. Camp near Bullen.[25]

On 9 September, along with the Earl of Hertford, the Bishop of Winchester and Sir William Paget, Rich met the French ambassadors at Hardelot Castle, at the request of the Privy Council, where they had dinner and discussed terms regarding the siege.[26]

Nearly a month later, the Privy Council sent instruction once more that Rich, Paulet and Sir John Gage were:

> to answer the emperor's ambassadors as follows: – 1. That the Emperor ought not, by the treaty, to have concluded peace without the common consent…2. Where Cardinal Turnon declared to the Emperor that the conditions required by the King were importable…3. The excuse for the not coming of the French ambassadors into England is feigned, for they were detained justly and with their own consents, given before the Council and the Duke of Alberkirk, and the King cannot but think that the French king will send his ambassadors into England, where they may have quicker expedition; but, if not, a commission is addressed to the Great Chamberlain, Winchester, Comptroller, Secretary Paget and Riche, with which the Great Chamberlain and Paget shall repair to Calais.[27]

Rich was finally sent money, £55,348 17*s* 3*d* (around £23,321,663 in today's money[28]) in October which was deemed enough to for an army of 4,200 men, not the 8,000 he was overseeing, and for just 14 days. The Council wrote to him once more asking for further explanation of the costs he had estimated for transportation soldiers and horses. These were estimated at 2s. per man[29], whereas Rich was asking for £6,000. On 8 October the Council asked him to 'send over with diligence a more plain and more certain declaration, as well of th'expenses already paid as of your remain and what shall be due at the next pay day…upon receipt whereof money shall be sent.'[30]

Rich's response to Cranmer, Wriothesley and St John a few days later attempted to detail his expenditure and the reasons for it:

> Encloses a brief declaration of such particular payments as he has made since 24 Sept., which was four or five days before the King left Boleyn. Had then in hand 16,000l. and afterwards received from Wotton of Calyce 12,000l. and out of England 33,333l. 6s. 8d. Cannot make a perfect declaration in so brief a time, but they shall have it in five or six days. Where they write that the King marvels at his asking 6,000l. for the transportation of 8,000 men; if that number is in the brief (fn. n6) enclosed in the Lords' letters the clerk was to blame, for in the writer's copy in his own hand there is no number. The 6,000l. was esteemed by the two vice-treasurers and Mr. Southwell's clerk to be the charge for the transportation of the army and for conduct money (which was esteemed at 5s. a man). At the making of the Lords' former letter many sick men remained here for lack of passage, "and also many horses, which we thought had been gone before my coming hither". Is sure that if they knew the diligence and policy used, they would think that he and the others did their duty. Cannot yet send the charges for next pay day, as the vice-treasurers cannot declare how many be gone and how many remain until a muster is taken, which the Lords here have ordered. The soldiers and most of their captains lie, in several places, five or six miles from Calais. Will make a full declaration when his clerks come, one of whom is left in Bullen to pay the money there, and the other gone into England for money. Begs despatch of his servants with money, for "the poor soldiers may very evil forbear their money, considering the scarcity of victual that is here".[31]

At the end of October, Rich detailed an account to the Lord Chancellor:

> sends a brief declaration of receipts and payments since 24 September, which was within five or six days before the King's departure from Bulloigne. Is anxious to declare his account. The books and warrants for his payments

> from 1 May to 9 July he thought not convenient to bring over sea; and they are at his house in London, with his commission. Begs that the King will appoint someone to take his account. Has of th'encrease of money about 1,300l. over and above the sum contained in the brief declaration but cannot tell the certainty of that because Freman and Highame are at their houses in England, who had charge of the receipt under him. Has laid out money for horses, wagons, etc, for conveyance of the King's treasure, whereof he has had yet no time to ask allowances. Has received no money from England since receipt of the 40,000 marks. Begs suit to the King for his return, as he has been "evil pained of the stone and ache in my back"; and there is no cause for his tarrying, as money may be left with the treasurer of Calice, or Sir Richard Southwell's clerk Myldemaye, or with the writer's clerk. Thus the King may be discharged of his poor diet, and himself the sooner rid of his account.[32]

Knowing the king did not like being made a fool of, Rich was desperate to prove he was not enriching himself at the king's expense during the French campaign. He knew it would not go well for him if the king decided he was no longer useful, especially when there were those in the court who would be happy to see him gone. After five months as treasurer in the French campaign, he resigned the post and returned to England in November, on the basis of ill health (his health would impact him at a later crisis). He had tried his best to explain his decisions, but once Henry had begun to question Rich's honesty in the matter, he knew it was best to get out while he had the chance.

In December that year Charles, Duke of Suffolk, President of the Council and Great Master of the Household, Sir John Baker, Chancellor of First Fruits and Tenths, Sir Edward North, Chancellor of Augmentations, and Sir Thomas Moyle, one of the General Surveyors, were given a commission to review the accounts of both Rich and Wriothesley, and also to discharge them from their positions.[33]

In addition to being paid for his services,[34] and having his costs covered, Rich was also given a commission:[35]

> to take possession of all lawful prizes captured by the Navy since the beginning of the wars against France and Scotland (except such as have already been disposed of by the King) and sell them to the King's profit, paying over the

> proceeds in "a grosse summe" to the Treasurer of the Chamber for the time being; also to compel, by imprisonment or otherwise, such as have embezzled or concealed prizes to account for them.[36]

In his capacity as Lieutenant in Essex, Rich also arranged for 30 men under his jurisdiction to be sent to Calais, with an additional 50 horsemen and 200 foot soldiers a few months later. Along with the Earl of Oxford, they were also responsible for coastal defences of Essex and Suffolk. Although he had been accused of not doing his job correctly while treasurer, Rich has managed to retain the king's trust.

* * *

It was during the French campaign that Rich acquired one of his most prized properties, the priory of St Bartholomew's in London, which he transformed into his London townhouse. The priory itself was closed down in 1539 during the dissolution, where it remained in the king's hands until Rich was granted it for a fee of 1,6041 11*s* 3*d* (roughly £676,000 in today's money[37]). Included in the grant was:

> the close there called Greate Saynte Bartholomews Close…all buildings within the site of the monastery…, all messuages… in le Churche Rowe. Paradyse, Petywales within the said Great Saynte Bartholomewes Close, five messuages and two stables in Westsmythfelde…, and an aqueduct running from a place called le Conduyt Hed of St. Bartholomewes within the manor of Canbery in Iseldon parish to the said priory and close.

He would also hold the grant for the annual St Bartholomew's fair.[38] As with Leighs, he had much of the site demolished for his townhouse to be built. Some of the church remains today, restored in the late 1800s, and the only glimpse of Rich's townhouse is a half-timbered house above the church's entrance. It is not certain that this was Rich's creation, and could have been added after it changed hands.

* * *

A few years later, in 1546, Rich was personally involved in the indefensible – and illegal – act of torturing a woman, Anne Askew. What made things worse was the fact the man who was supposed to be carrying the torture refused, leaving Rich and Thomas Wriothesley (Lord Chancellor) to use the apparatus themselves.

Anne Askew, whose married name was Kyme, was born around 1521. As she reached adulthood, she had turned towards the Protestant religion, but unlike others who had done the same, was very open about it. Born near Grimsby, her marriage had been arranged by her parents and was an unhappy one. Anne was well educated and interested in the teachings of the Bible, most specifically of evangelicals, and began to share her views with the world, whether it wanted to hear them or not. Her husband was so frustrated with her preaching that he threw her out. Anne sought a divorce, before leaving for London, where she had family connections with the nobles and gentry of the court, especially that of Queen Katheryn Parr's ladies. She first came to the attention of the authorities in March 1545 and was questioned by Bishop Bonner as she was now a person of interest to the Catholic faction of the court due to her connections to the queen.

In May 1546, her and her estranged husband were called to the king's council, and after refusing to acknowledge him as her husband, she was interrogated for a number of days in an attempt to persuade her to convert back to religious conservatism. She was also pressed on her connection to members of the queen's court, including the Countess of Hertford, Lady Denny, and the Duchess of Suffolk. She was taken to Newgate Prison and eventually arraigned for heresy, before being confined to the Tower (secretly to begin with). She would go down in history as one of only two women (on record) subjected to torture in the Tower and burnt at the stake.

Although torture seems barbaric to us today, by medieval standards it was an accepted fact that it was, at times, was necessary during interrogations in order to secure valuable information, or a confession. Though illegal under common law, it was permitted in cases of treason or other offences against the State, if approved by the king or by his Privy council.[39] The Council books during the time of Henry VIII 'afford the most unequivocal evidence of the practice of torture during the period to which they refer Registers of the proceedings of the Privy Council [...] in these books there are numerous

Sir Richard Rich by Hans Holbein c.1532–43. The only contemporary image of Richard Rich, most likely done to celebrate his rise in the elite of Tudor society. Thought to be part of a pair, the other being of his wife. This sketch would have most likely been used for a full-coloured painting. (*Wikimedia Commons public domain*)

Elizabeth, Lady Rich (née Jenks) by Hans Holbein, c.1532–43. As with her husband's portrait, this is the only known contemporary image of Elizabeth. She would have been wearing her finest clothes to show of her wealth and status. (*Wikimedia Commons public domain*)

King Henry VIII by Hans Holbein, date unknown. The first Tudor monarch who Rich served under (and very loyally). Rich knew in order to survive the court he needed to give the king what he wanted, even if it meant bending the rules. (*Wikimedia Commons public domain*)

King Edward VI, attributed to William Scrots, c.1546. Under the young King Edward, Rich would reach the zenith of his power by being made Lord Chancellor. However, this was most likely due to the friends he had who were close to the king rather than because of the young king's trust in Rich. (*Wikimedia Commons public domain*)

Queen Mary I, Hans Eworth. Although Mary brought Eng-land back to the Catholic faith, and Rich was able to openly practise his religion once more, he found himself at odds with his queen as he did not want to return the church lands he had purchased during the Reformation. This did not stop him actively persecuting 'heretics' in his home county of Essex. (*Wikimedia Commons public domain*)

Queen Elizabeth I, Clopton Portrait c.1558 and 1650. Rich would be graced with a visit from Queen Elizabeth just after she became Queen. She was the fourth monarch he would serve under although only briefly as he died on 12th June, 1567, at 71 years of age. (*Wikimedia commons public domain*)

Thomas More by Hans Holbein, 1527. It is thought that Rich and More may have known each other before the latter became Lord Chancellor under Henry VIII. Although he may have respected Rich as a fellow law student, he did not consider him a friend, and this was further shown during his imprisonment in the Tower and the infamous 'conversation' that took place between the pair, which gave Henry VIII the 'evidence' he needed to have his former friend beheaded. This is one of the main reasons for Rich's villainous reputation today.It is thought that Rich and More may have known each other before the latter became Lord Chancellor under Henry VIII. Although he may have respected Rich as a fellow law student, he did not consider him a friend, and this was further shown during his imprisonment in the Tower and the infamous 'conver-sation' that took place between the pair, which gave Henry VIII the 'evidence' he needed to have his former friend beheaded. This is one of the main reasons for Rich's villainous reputation today. (*Wikimedia Commons public domain*)

Thomas Audley, Earl of Arundel, unknown artist and date. Gaining the patronage of Audley allowed Rich to progress his career in the Tudor court, leading to his becoming Chancellor of the Court of Augmentations and Lord Chancellor. Both their careers followed a similar path, though Audley never fully rose to the same heights as Rich and some of his other contemporaries. (*Wikimedia Commons public domain*)

The Gatehouse, Leez Priory. The largest remaining part of the Priory that Rich would have recognised. This would have been the inner entrance for those visiting Rich, and presented the opportunity for him to show his wealth. (*Photo by the author*)

Leez Priory, 2025. Leez Priory, once Rich's great home, as it is today. Some features still remain which Rich would recognise, including the gatehouse. (*Photo by the author*)

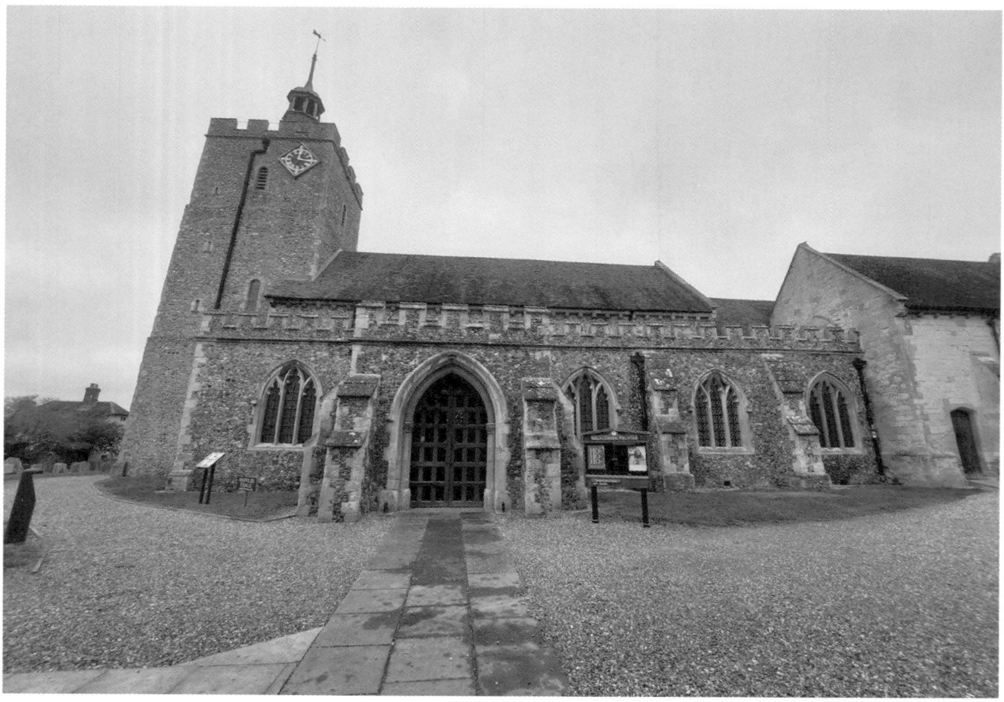

Holy Cross Church, Felsted, Essex 2025. The site of the final resting place of Richard Rich. (*Photo by the author*)

Richard Rich Tomb, Holy Cross Church, Felsted, Essex 2025. This is the only other confirmed image of Rich. His tomb was built around 1620 and though it may not bear much likeness, it was thought appropriate at the time. (*Photo by the author*)

Thomas Wriothesley, Hans Holbein c.1536-40. Another peer of Rich's, Wriothesley was another who survived the truing of King Henry VIII, but he fell from power and never regained his position. Rich would be the one to replace him as Lord Chancellor. (*Wikimedia Commons public domain*)

Thomas Cromwell, by Hans Holbein, 1532–3. Rich and Cromwell worked alongside one another, with Cromwell placing Rich has Chancellor of the Court of Augmentations. It was this role that made Rich a very wealthy man. However, when the king moved against Cromwell, Rich turned against his former boss. (*Wikimedia Commons public domain*)

Anne Askew, Hans Eworth, 1560. Anne was very strong in her beliefs and found herself being questioned and eventually tortured by Rich and Wriothesley in the hope that she would incriminate her fellow Reformist, Queen Katheryn Parr. Anne was later burned at the stake. (*Wikimedia Commons public domain*)

The Rich Coat of Arms. (*Wikimedia Commons*)

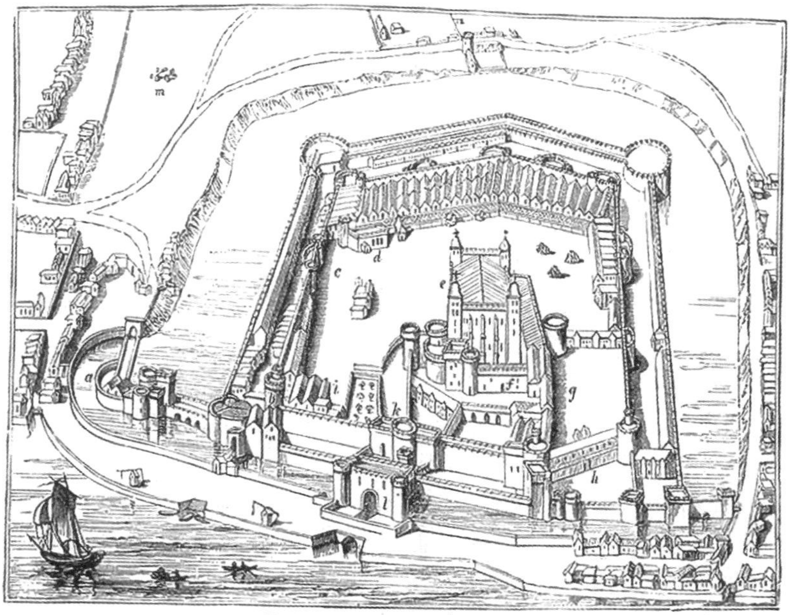

PLAN OF THE TOWER OF LONDON.

a. Lion's Tower.
b. Bell Tower.
c. Beauchamp Tower.
d. The Chapel.
e. The Keep, or White Tower.
f. Jewel House.
g. Queen's Lodgings.
h. Queen's Gallery and Garden.
i. Lieutenant's Lodgings.
k. Bloody Tower.
l. St. Thomas' Tower, and Traitor's Gate.
m. Place of Execution on Tower-hill.

The Tower of London, *Picturesque England* by Laura Valentine, based on an engraving published in 1597. Rich was familiar with the Tower but was never imprisoned there, unlike a number of his peers.

The Family of Henry VIII, Yale Centre for British Art c.1590. King Henry VIII and his three children, including Mary's husband, James I. Rich served under all of these monarchs. (*Wikimedia Commons public domain*)

Rochford Hall, 2017. Another home of Richard Rich, and the place where he died. (*Photo by the author*)

Site of public execution, Tower Hill 2025. The site of Tower Hill, just outside the Tower of London, where both Thomas More and Thomas Cromwell were beheaded. (*Photo by the author*)

Robert Rich, the tomb of Richard Rich, 2025. Rich's second son, and the one to inherit his title and estate, was not of a similar nature to his father, and did not excel in his political career. (*Photo by the author*)

entries of warrants from the Council authorizing the application of torture for the purpose of compelling the disclosure of political conspiracies and crimes of various descriptions In order to establish the truth.' Even Cromwell himself used torture to gain confessions,[40] so Rich and Wriothesley were not behaving completely beyond the limits of prevailing standards. It was simply the fact that they tortured a woman that was so shocking to many.

Evidence of Rich and Wriothesley's brutality survives today in the form of an account written by Askew herself and smuggled out from the Tower. After various interrogations, during which Anne reiterated her beliefs, she was condemned as a heretic at the Guildhall on 18 June 1546. She denied the charge:

> They said to me there, that I was a heretic, and condemned by the law, if I would stand in my opinion. I answered that I was no heretic, nor deserved any death by the law of God. But, as concerning the faith which I uttered and wrote to the council, I would not, I said, deny it, because I knew it was true. From here, she did not return to Newgate where she had initially been held but was taken to 'the sign of the Crown, where Master Rich, and the bishop of London, with all their power and flattering words, went about to persuade me from God [...] Then Master Rich sent me to the Tower, where I remained till three o'clock.[41]

It was thought by some of those in the Catholic faction – which at the time included Rich, and was headed by Gardiner and Wriothesley – that she may be able to incriminate Queen Kathryn Parr, or at least her ladies. Like a number of those in the court, Kathryn identified as a reformist and this was well known. It was clear to all those in the court that the king would not be around for much longer and that his young son Edward would be the next monarch, and whoever controlled him would be the power behind the throne. Edward's uncles, Edward and Thomas Seymour, were Reformists and still close to King Henry, but Kathryn was also stepmother to the prince. If she fell, then perhaps the Catholics would seize control and the king would leave his son in their hands. Rich and Wriothesley needed evidence to bring about Kathryn's downfall, and it was most likely because of this that Anne Askew was being held in the Tower.

Then came Rich and one of the councils, charging me upon my obedience, to show unto them, if I knew any man or woman of my sect. My answer was, that I knew none. Then they asked me of my Lady of Suffolk, my Lady of Sussex, my Lady of Hertford, my Lady Denny, and my Lady Fitzwilliam. To whom I answered, if I should pronounce any thing against them, that I were not able to prove it. Then said they unto me, that the king was informed that I could name, if I would, a great number of my sect. I answered that the king was as well deceived on that behalf, as disassembled in other matters...Then they said that there were diverse gentlewomen that gave me money: but I did not know their names. Then they said that there were diverse ladies that had sent me money. I answered, that there was a man in a blue coat who delivered me ten shillings, and said that my Lady of Hertford wait me; and another in a violet coat gave me eight shillings, and said my Lady Denny sent it me: whether it were true or no, I cannot tell; for I am not sure who sent it me, but as the maid did say. Then they said, there were members of the council that did maintain me: and I said, No.

Then they did put me on the rack, because I confessed no ladies or gentlewomen to be of my opinion, and thereon they kept me a long time; and because I lay still, and did not cry, my lord chancellor and Master Rich took pains to rack me with their own hands, till I was nigh dead.

Then the lieutenant caused me to be loose from the rack. Incontinently I swooned, and then they recovered me again. After that I sat for two long hours arguing with my lord chancellor upon the bare floor; where he, with many flattering words, persuaded me to leave my opinion. But my Lord God (I thank his everlasting goodness) gave me grace to persevere, and will do, I hope, to the very end.

Then I was brought to a house, and laid in a bed, with as weary and painful bones as ever had patient Job; I thank my Lord God there-for. Then my lord chancellor sent me word, if I would leave my opinion, I would want nothing: if I would not, I should forthwith to Newgate, and so be burned. I sent him again a word, that I would rather die, than break my faith.[42]

In the meantime, while they were making their way by land, the good lieutenant, eftsoons taking boat, sped him to the court in all haste to speak with the king before the others, and so did; who there making his humble suit to the king, desired his pardon, and showed him the whole matter as it stood...he...could not find in his heart to do, and therefore humbly craved his Highness's pardon. When the king had understood, he seemed not very well to like their so extreme handling of the woman, and also granted to the lieutenant his pardon, willing him to return and see to his charge.

Anne was brought to Smithfield to be burned on 16 July 1546, not far from Rich's house. She was carried in a chair due to the horrific ordeal she had endured at the Tower. Even at the end she was still promoting her religious beliefs and did not falter. She and two others were tied to stakes and burned in front of a crowd, which included Wriothesley, Norfolk and others.

Askew did not implicate Katheryn or her ladies in any way, causing frustration in the Catholic camp. They changed tack and started to look for evidence elsewhere. They knew that Kathryn had forbidden books in her possession, which the king would not be pleased about, and if they could locate these then the king could not ignore their complaints. They focused their energies on her ladies in the hope that they would betray Katheryn's trust. Among them were her sister, Lady Herbert, and two of her cousins, Lady Lane and Lady Tyrwhitt, all of whom were members of her privy chamber. It was thought if these three women could be questioned over their behaviour towards the Act of Six articles, then their apartments could be searched, and the banned books would be found. This plan, however, was stopped before it could be carried out.

Wriothesley, Gardiner and others including Rich looked for other ways to get Henry to agree to a warrant being issued against Katheryn. Their chance came one evening during the king's regular conversations with his queen, which were designed to take his mind off his painful leg. During this conversation, which was witnessed by Wriothesley, Katheryn spoke openly about her beliefs. Afterwards, Wriothesley approached the king and pointed out to him that his own wife was dictating what he should believe. This was enough for Henry, and he agreed to an arrest warrant being issued. Katheryn somehow found out about this. A copy of the Bill of Articles against her, which had been signed by Henry, was delivered to her apartment, sending her into a panic. On hearing that Katheryn was unwell, Foxe's account (John Foxe, was a clergyman and historian who authored *The Book of Martyrs*) says the king sent his physician, Dr Wendy, to see what was wrong and he secretly revealed what was afoot. Others suggest that Wendy was sent by the king to tell Katheryn all, possibly as a show of strength for the benefit of Katheryn and also the Catholic faction. Either way, Dr Wendy was a fellow reformer and warned her of the danger. She knew Henry did not make idle threats – two of his previous wives had met their fate on the scaffold. On hearing the news that Kathryn was distraught:

> the king, hearing what perplexity she was in, almost to the peril and danger of her life, sent his physicians unto her; who, travailing about her, and seeing what extremity she was in, did what they could for her recovery [...] Dr Wendy advised Katherine to use, all secrecy in that behalf, and exhorting her somewhat to frame and conform herself unto the king's mind, saying, he did not doubt but, if she would so do, and show her humble submission unto him, she should find him gracious and favourable unto her.[43]

Kathryn knew how to appease Henry and appeal to his ego. When the king came to see her in her bed, she confessed to him that she feared he had taken displeasure with her and had utterly forsaken her. Henry responded that she had not done so and calmed Katheryn's nerves. However, she knew she was still in danger. She wasted no time and had her ladies remove any potentially dangerous books to her uncle's home. She then attempted convince the king she was not against him.

> She went to the King the following evening, she entered a conversation with him on religion and reminded him she knew of her place as a woman and your Majesty being so excellent in gifts and ornaments of wisdom, and I a silly poor woman, so much inferior in all respects of nature unto you [...] Henry then attempted to bait Kathryn as her words were different than the conversations that they had had previous where he felt she was in effect instructing him in religion.[44]

She knew that she had overstepped the mark with the king and was being punished for it, and chose her words carefully:

> If your Majesty take it so...then hath your Majesty very much mistaken me, who have ever been of the opinion, to think it very unseemly, and preposterous, for the woman to take upon her the office of an instructor or teacher to her lord and husband; but rather to learn of her husband, and to be taught by him. And whereas I have, with your Majesty's leave, heretofore been bold to hold talk with your Majesty, wherein sometimes in opinions there hath seemed some difference, I have not done it so much to maintain opinion, as I did it rather to minister talk, not only to the end your Majesty might with less grief pass over this painful time of your infirmity, being attentive to our talk, and hoping that your Majesty should reap some ease thereby; but also that I, hearing your Majesty's learned discourse, might receive to myself some profit thereby.[45]

She had been trying to keep his mind away from the pain in his leg, and had wanted to learn from him. She was never trying to instruct him. He was her lord and husband. How could he think that? Kathryn had flattered the king, calmed his mind, and reminded him of her love for him. Henry, whether he believed this or not, most likely did not want to go through the pain of losing another wife. He was old, tired, and ill, and in Kathryn he had a loving spouse.

> "And is it even so, sweetheart!" quoth the king, "and tended your arguments to no worse end? Then, perfect friends we are now again, as ever at any time heretofore." And as he sat in his chair, embracing her in his arms, and kissing her, he added this, saying, that it did him better at that time to hear those words of her own mouth, than if he had heard present news of a hundred thousand pounds in money fallen unto him.[46]

The crisis had been averted, although no one told Gardiner and Wriothesley. When Wriothesley approached Kathryn the following day with the arrest warrant, accompanied by 40 guards, the king humiliated him:

> His demur of happiness and mirth with Kathryn changed and turning towards his lord chancellor Wriothesley he called him a Knave! With other words including beast and fol. And with that the king commanded him presently to avaunt out of his presence. Which words, although they were uttered somewhat low, yet were they so vehemently whispered out by the king, that the queen did easily, with her ladies aforesaid, overhear them; which had been not a little to her comfort, if she had known at that time the whole cause of his coming, as perfectly as after she knew it. Thus departed the lord chancellor out of the king's presence as he came, with all his train; the whole mould of all his device being utterly broken.[47]

As with Kathryn the king had put Wriothesley in his place. It was now clear to all in court, whatever their beliefs, that Henry was still in charge.

* * *

After Cromwell's fall, Rich aligned himself with the Catholic faction. It seemed that there was a chance of their being the dominant power for a time and Rich was most likely appeased in his soul to be persecuting heretics who were against the Catholic church. Like the rest of the court, he knew the king was not going to live for much longer. He decided to play it safe and reach out to those in the Protestant camp, like the Seymours, in the hope that whoever held the power after Henry's death would consider him a useful ally, albeit an untrustworthy one.

On 2 December 1546, Henry Howard[48] was arrested on charges of treason. His father, Thomas, was arrested later:

> I, Thomas duke of Norfolke do confess and knowledge myself to have offended the King in opening his secret counsels at divers times to sundry persons [...] I have concealed high treason in keeping secret the false acts of my son [...] I confess my crime no less than high treason and, although I do not deserve it, humbly beg his Highness to have pity upon me, and I shall daily pray to God for the preservation of his noble succession [...] subscribed by me in the presence of the Lord Wriothesley, ...Lord St. John... the earl of Harteforde...Sir Anthonye Browne...Sir William Paggete ...Sir Richard Riche, Sir John Baker.[49]

Rich was even present when Norfolk confessed his and his son's crimes, purely in the role as member of the Privy Council. And though there was plotting involved in their downfall, most likely headed by the Seymours, Rich was not directly involved. Thomas Howard, 3rd Duke of Norfolk, was cousin to Anne Boleyn, and was a great and powerful figure in the Tudor court. He at times had angered the king, who did not forget those who had gone against him or who could pose a threat to him. First, Norfolk's son, Henry Howard, was arrested and charged with treasonably quartering the royal arms. Norfolk was later arrested after his former friend Richard Southwell gave evidence against him. The Seymours and the Protestant faction jumped at the chance to try and topple a threat to their own power and influence. Another reason for Norfolk's fall from grace was his disdain towards the new men in court, those who had risen to power and were not born into the gentry. He referred to Cromwell as a 'foul churl', and Paget a 'mean creature'. Norfolk was the one responsible for Cromwell's fall and now found himself in the same position, though this was due to the actions of his son. Henry Howard was executed on 19 January 1547. Norfolk, due to be executed on 28 of January, survived only because the king died in the early hours of that day.[50]

* * *

Henry VIII had ruled England for nearly 38 years, during which time men and women rose with his favour and fell, some meeting an untimely death. Many noble families did not survive his reign without having suffered some loss or arrest. However, a small number in the king's favour grew rich and remained in their positions at his death: one of these men was Richard Rich.

On Henry's death Rich did not hold a major office, but he never entered the Tower nor faced imprisonment while serving under the king. He played his cards well. Rich was awarded 661 13*s* 4*d* annually [approximately £181,621 in today's money[51]] from Henry's will, and was included in a list of persons to assist the appointed council advising Edward until he came of age.

> Charging his said son to be ruled as regards marriage and all affairs by the aforesaid Councillors…Archbishop of Canterbury, the Lord Wriothesley,… the Lord St. John,… the Earl of Hertford… the Lord Russell,…the Viscount Lisle,…the bishop Tunstall of Duresme, Sir Anthony Broun,…Sir Edward Montagu,…Justice Bromley, Sir Edward North,…Sir William Paget,… Sir Anthony Denny and Sir William Harbard,…Sir Edward Wootton and Dr. Wootton his brother…until he has completed his eighteenth year. And the following persons shall be of Council for the assistance of the foresaid Councillors when required, viz., the present earls of Arundel and Essex, Sir Thomas Cheney,…Sir John Gage,…Sir Anthony Wingfield, … Sir William Petre, one of our two principal secretaries, Sir Richard Rich, Sir John Baker, Sir Ralph Sadleyr, Sir Thomas Seymour, Sir Richard Southwell, and Sir Edmond Peckham.
>
> In token of special love and favour, these Councillors and servants shall receive as follows… the earl of Arundell, Lord Chamberlain, Sir Anthony Wingfeld, Sir Edm. Peckham, Sir Richard Rich, Sir John Bak[er] and Sir Richard Southwell, each 200l., Westminster Palace, 30 Dec. 1546[52]'

The reign of Henry Tudor was over, and England now entered the reign of King Edward VI, a boy of only nine years old. Before Henry's death, those who held power in the court found themselves siding with the Catholic faction or the reformers. After his death, factions and 'friendships' became mixed once more. For a man like Rich, he would follow those who kept him in a position of wealth and influence, even if it was the reformers, and he would find himself at the top of the food chain in the Tudor court.

Lord Chancellor

Edward Tudor, now King Edward VI, was crowned at Westminster Abbey on 20 February 1547. Under his father's orders, Edward's rule was to be overseen by nominated councillors, however, this decision was soon changed. After agreement by those who had been appointed to govern the young king, it was decided that Edward Seymour, uncle to the young king and Lord Protector Somerset, would take control. It was under Somerset's rule that Rich was appointed a member of the king's council. Somerset was no doubt appointing men he could trust, but why he thought Rich fitted the bill is unclear, especially after his involvement with the attempted downfall of Kathryn Parr. Maybe Somerset knew Rich would be loyal to those who did not threaten his wealth and status. Rich did his best to remain on good terms with Seymour and some other members of the Protestant faction. He had been in the game long enough to know how to survive. He had been one of the counsellors charged with questioning the Duke of Norfolk and his son, the Earl of Surrey, when they were arrested towards the end of Henry VIII's reign, and he most likely used this to show his loyalty was not with the Catholic faction.

On 25 February 1547, Rich was created a baron as part of the late king's wishes. He was also granted lands with a grant worth £66 13*s.* 4*d.* per annum. He would now, by virtue of his office, take a prominent part in the Privy Council. He was not, however, confirmed until 30 November.

* * *

Rich was one of those placed in charge of arranging the coronation of the new young king. This would have included arranging the procession from the Tower of London to the Palace of Westminster on 19 February. On the day of his coronation, Edward travelled by barge to the Court of Augmentations in Whitehall and from there to Westminster Abbey, where the service was officiated by Cranmer.

In his will, Henry had appointed 16 people to sit on a council to run the country until the young Edward came of age at 18. One third of those on the committee were those of the nobility and ancient lineage, the rest were, like Rich, men who had advanced through their own skills and merit. These various committees included one to hear suits of the common law, one to look at the state of the courts, a committee of defence, a committee for the state, and a committee for the calling of forfeits done against the laws, and one for the punishing of the breakers of proclamations.[1] Along with Rich and Edward Seymour, the others on the council included the Bishop of Canterbury, the Duke of Northumberland (John Dudley), the Marquess of Northampton (William Parr), the Earl of Pembroke (brother-in-law to Kathryn Parr), the Lord Admiral (Thomas Seymour), William Cecil, Sir John Gage, Sir Walter Mildmay. All of them were of the Reformist persuasion, and, at first, supporters of Somerset.[2]

* * *

Rich's career until this point had been advancing, and he had been making connections since his time at the Inns of Court. He now reached one of the highest positions in court in 1548, that of Lord Chancellor, after the previous occupant, Thomas Wriothesley, was removed from his post, likely due to the involvement of others (including Rich).

Wriothesley had been appointed as Chancellor in April 1544 by King Henry VIII. An acute and irascible man, Wriothesley took personal satisfaction in destroying the careers of others, and of being a bully when questioning the likes of Catherine Howard, Anne Askew, and the Earl of Surrey (to name just a few).[3] Born 21 December 1505, into a family with royal connections, Wriothesley started his career in the service of Stephen Gardiner, before transferring his service to Cromwell. His career started to improve, and he rose to become Cromwell's chief clerk and personal secretary by May 1530. Cromwell, it seemed, recognised someone, like himself, with ambition and a acute political acumen. However, like most, Wriothesley would turn against

Cromwell, and even spoke against him to Henry when it was clear the king was turning against his unofficial second in command.

In 1533, Wriothesley married Jane Cheyne, Gardiner's niece and a wealthy heiress. Another member of the gentry to profit from the dissolution, Wriothesley would acquire properties in Hampshire, amongst others, transforming Titchfield abbey into a luxurious primary residence for himself and his growing family. Historian Elton states that he was manifestly the most successful civil servant of his day, and, in a way, the head of the civil service in the latter 1530s.[4] After Cromwell's fall he realigned himself with Gardiner (he may even played a part in Cromwell's demise) and became one of the leading men of the court. He was a true Henrician who would have nothing to do with the Pope and welcomed the dissolution of the monasteries, but he remained a religious conservative. Historian Alison Weir describes him as being able, enterprising, tenacious and ruthless, yet insufferably overconfident and egotistic.[5]

Towards the end of King Henry's reign, Wriothesley rose even higher, being made a baron in January 1544.[6] A few months later in April he was appointed the Lord Chancellor.[7] It was during this period that he was one of the key figures in the torture of Anne Askew, and in the attempt to have Kathryn Parr arrested. Wriothesley hoped that his lofty position in the court would continue under the new young king. However, he soon realised that it was Somerset who now pulled the strings, and who was also starting to resent him and his religious views. In an attempt to appease him, Somerset made Wriothesley the Earl of Southampton on 16 February 1547, but this was not enough. In 1545, Wriothesley had already raised his concerns about Somerset's greed to Henry, but the king had not heeded his warning. Now seeing him gain more power by being appointed Lord Protector, Wriothesley was even more concerned and started to speak out. In an attempt to silence him, Somerset started to look for a way to ruin the Lord Chancellor, and he employed Rich to help.

It would not just be Wriothesley who would find his fortunes had changed. Others in the Catholic/conservative faction, like Bishop Gardiner, the other leading member, was imprisoned in the Tower. Wriothesley found himself accused of issuing a commission without warrant,[8] and was removed as Lord Chancellor and placed under house arrest at his

London townhouse in Ely Place. It seemed that Wriothesley was diverting business to chancery from the common law courts. Some students of the Inns of Court discovered this and raised it with Somerset, who started an investigation, led by Rich. Not surprisingly, the commission came back stating he had encroached on common law and had 'altered and violated by reason of Decrees made in the Saide Courte'. In their report, Rich and the six other appointees stated that, as a result of his crimes, Wriothesley had forfeited his office of Chancellor and 'incurred the dangers penalties and paynes as it shall please…the said Lord Protector and Counsil to set upon him for the same and also imprisonment of his body at the King's[9] will.' He was forced to surrender the Great Seal.

Eventually released from arrest, Wriothesley was restored to the council but not the chancellorship. He thought his chances would improve when he was involved with the fall of Somerset and the rise of Dudley, but he was wrong. Those around him, including Rich, conspired to have Wriothesley removed from court for good, though his staunch Catholicism probably did him no favours. To prevent him from causing more trouble he was threatened with imprisonment and fines if he objected. Reluctantly, Wriothesley accepted his fate, but his health began to fail and he died on 30 July 1550.[10]

Finally, it was Rich's turn to be appointed Lord Chancellor, on 23 October 1548. It was a role that both More and Cromwell had held until their deaths (which Rich had played a big part in). His duties included opening parliament at the official state opening, and instructing the commons to appoint a speaker, a role that Rich himself had held at one time. The role would also include being Keeper of the King's Great Seal, which was given to him a few days later on the 26th. As Chancellor, he would begin to withdraw from council meetings in order to concentrate on the revenue and expenses of the royal household, something that Rich was certainly well qualified to do. The appointment was a reward for his loyalty to Somerset. Rich would also be involved in Somerset's decision to repeal some of the treason laws,[11] which had been changed during Henry VIII's reign, and secured for himself a private act guaranteeing certain lands.

* * *

Under Edward and Somerset, England had entered a period of religious change once more, moving the country further away from the Henrician Catholic stance. English subjects were now to adopt the Protestant faith. The Book of Common Prayer was introduced, making it illegal to hear the Latin Mass, and Protestant services were read out in church. Rich, in his role as Chancellor, fully backed Somerset's move towards Protestantism. He requested that the bishops adopt the new rites ordained by the prayer book of 1549, and instructed local justices to make sure that people adopted the new practices and did not speak out against them.[12]

His role as Chancellor also meant questioning a former colleague, and maybe sometime friend, Stephen Gardiner, who was arrested in 1547 for not agreeing to the new Book of Common Prayer. A year later, while still imprisoned in the Tower, Gardiner was visited by Rich and others, who tried to get him to conform to the new book. Gardiner refused, telling Rich he would suffer punishment if need be. He was told he would have a proper hearing, but another year passed before anything happened. He was released in January 1548 and faced further house arrest at Southwark palace.

It seemed Rich showed some loyalty towards his former Catholic peers. In 1551, when Stephen Gardiner was put on trial, Rich was called as a witness for the prosecution. The trial was headed by Cranmer, starting at Lambeth, and its eighth session was held at Rich's house at St Bartholomew's. Gardiner faced 19 charges, against which he defended himself to the best of his ability. Of course, Rich did his duty, but it was evident he was reluctant to speak against Gardiner.[13] Following the trial Gardiner was confined in the Tower and had his bishopric removed.

Another who refused to follow Edward VI and Seymour's new religious beliefs was the king's own sister, Mary. After reconciling in 1536, Mary had been left alone by her father and when her brother came to the throne nothing really changed for her. She was still openly attending mass, despite her brother's orders, which she ignored.

Initially Edward, or more likely Somerset and the council, decided to attempt a soft approach towards her. She had been invited by Rich to stay at his home on 28 July 1550[14] in order to join him on hunting trips and other sporting events,[15] in addition to invitations to court and another invite to his home on 13 August, which later had to be cancelled as Rich 'fell sore sike, with 40 more of his house, so that the lady Mary came not thither *at that time.'[16] These invites could have been suggested by Rich, as he was, at heart, a Catholic as well, but Mary was not stupid and knew it was an attempt to try and persuade her to change her beliefs. Mary was even invited to visit her brother in court, but refused for fear of becoming trapped there. 'The lady Mary after long communication was content to come to Leis to the lord chauncelour, and then to Hunsdon, but she utterly denied coming to the court or Oking at that time.[17] She tried various excuses to turn down the request and eventually the council left her be.[18]

The following year, however, the king's approach towards his sister hardened. Rich was sent to Mary's home of Copthall in Essex, on 28 August 1552, to inform her of her brother's order that she cease to celebrate Mass. Accompanying him was Sir Anthony Wingfield, Comptroller of the King's household, and Sir William Petre, principal secretary to the king. Rich was not given a warm welcome. In fact, he was refused entry to her home and Mary shouted insults at him from a balcony, 'You given me fair words but your deed be always ill towards me.'[19] She may have even been more hostile towards him due to his betrayal of the Catholic faith, and it was clear by her words that she did not trust him. While there, Mary was also informed that Sir Anthony Wingfield would be replacing Robert Rochester as her comptroller. As with her father, she was being dictated to, but this time it seems she was going to fight back rather than despair and live in fear.

It is interesting to note that Rich and Lady Mary were not enemies, and Rich may have even been inclined towards her cause. However, he had been ordered by his king to do a job, and, like his former colleague Cromwell, he did not let his friendships get in the way of the king's orders.

After their visit, Rich, Wingfield and Petre reported what had happened in a letter to the king and Privy Council:

> A Note of the Report of the Message done to the Lady Mary's Grace by us…First having received Commandment and Instructions from the King's Majesty, we repaired to the said Lady Mary's house at Copped Hall in Essex .I the Lord Chancellor delivered his Majesty's Letters to her, which she received upon her knees, saying that for honour of the King's Majesty's hand, wherewith the said Letters were signed, she would kiss the Letter;

and not for their matter contained in them, for the matter, said she, I take to proceed not from his Majesty but from you his Council…we told her at good length how the King's Majesty having used all the gentle means and exhortations that he might to have reduced her to the Rites of Religion and Order of Divine service set forth by the laws of the realm, and finding her nothing conformable, but still remaining in her former error, had resolved by the whole estate of his Majesty's Privy Council, and with the consent of divers others of the Nobility, that she should no longer use the private Mass, nor any other divine Service than is set forth by the Laws of the Realm… We told her further that the King's Majesty's pleasure was we should also give strait charge to her Chaplains, that none of them should presume to say any Mass, or other divine service than is set forth by the Laws of the Realm, and like charge to all her servants that none of them shulde presume to hear any Mass, or other divine service than is aforesaid. Hereunto her answer was thus. First, she protested that to the King's Majesty she was, is, and ever will be his Majesty's most humble and most obedient subject and poor Sister, and would most willingly obey all his commandments in any thing (her conscience saved,) yea and would willingly and gladly suffer death to do his Majesty's good; but rather than she will agree to use any other service than which used at the death of the late King her father, she would lay her head on a block and suffer death. But, she said, I am unworthy to suffer death in such a good quarrel. When the King's Majesty (said she) shall come to such years that he may be able to judge these things himself, his Majesty shall find me ready to obey his orders in religion, but now in these years, although he good sweet King have more knowledge than any other of his years, yet is it not possible that he can be a judge in these things…And, quoth she…I will protest openly that you of the Council are the cause of my death; you give me fair words but your deeds are always ill towards me. And having said thus, she departed from us into her bedchamber, and delivered to me the Lord Chancellor a RING, upon her knees, most humbly, with very humble recommendations, saying that she would die his true subject and sister, and obey his Commandments in all things except in these matters of Religion, touching the Mass and the new service. But yet, said she, this shall never be told to the King's Majesty… Finally when we had said and done as is aforesaid, and were gone out of the house…the Lady Mary's Grace sent to us to speak with her one word at a window. When we came into the Court, notwithstanding that we offered to come up to her chamber, she would need to speak out of the window, and prayed us to speak to the Lords of the Council that her comptroller might shortly return.[20]

As to where Rich's Catholic loyalties lay in his involvement with Mary, it is clear they were certainly non-existent in the public eye. He chose to follow the king's and Somerset's direction, especially when it came to Mary refusing to cease hearing Mass. He would be present at the council in March 1550 where Sir Anthony Browne was sent to Fleet prison for hearing Mass, and he was on the council once more in April 1551, when her chaplain, Dr Mallet, was sent to the Tower for saying Mass.

Rich was involved in the questioning and imprisonment of Edmund Bonner in 1549. Bonner, who was until his arrest The Bishop of London, had spoken out against the Book of Common Prayer and the Act of Uniformity and was placed in Marshalsea Prison. On 7 February 1550 he was called before the King's Council at Westminster about how

> he had used in his sermon and examination at Lambeth afore my Lord of Canterbury, which he could not deny, and for his contempt deprived by the Bishop of Canterbury from his bishopric, which sentence this day all the Counsaill by the mouth of the Lord Chancellor of England confirmed, and so my Lord Chancellor commanded him to be had from thence to the place he came from, there to remain in perpetual prison at the King's pleasure, and to lose all his spiritual promotions and dignities for ever.[21]

Banner was released on the ascension of Mary and restored to his bishopric.

Rich's role in attacking Catholics did not stop there. He was involved in questioning Joan Boucher, an Anabaptist who was burnt at the stake on 2 May 1550 at Smithfield. She was arrested as a heretic in 1548 and charged the following April, but was not burnt until a year later. It was hoped that during that time she would recant. It is said King Edward did not want to sign her death warrant but was pushed to do so by Cranmer. Edward then laid her death at Cranmer's door.

> He always spared and favoured the life of man; as once appeared in a certain dissertation of his had with Master Cheek, in favouring the life of heretics; insomuch that when Joan Bocher should be burned, all the council could not move him to put to his hand, but were fain to get DR Cranmer to persuade with him, and yet neither could he, with much labour, induce the king so to do; saying, "What, my Lord? will ye have me to send her quick to the devil

> in her error" So that DR Cranmer himself confessed, that he had never so much to do in all his life, as to cause the king to put to his hand, saying that he would lay all the charge thereof upon Cranmer before God.[22]

Rich would be tasked with holding her at his home in York place, where he 'had her a sevenight in my house after the writ was it for her to be burnt where my lord of canterbury and the bishop ridley related almost daily into her.'[23] As Lord Chancellor Rich was responsible for enacting the punishments to those who went against the king's religious policies, and this included anyone from Catholics to those on the opposite side, including Anabaptists.

* * *

Although the actions discussed above were endorsed by the young king, it cannot be ignored that he was guided and counselled by his uncle, Edward Seymour. Edward Seymour, born c.1500 to Sir John Seymour and Margery Wentworth, both from Suffolk. He rose in the ranks, like his colleagues, including William Parr and Wriothesley, and was rewarded for his skills as an ambassador, soldier and politician. Though his progress was helped by the fact that his sister was married to the king in 1536. After her death he was able to keep his position in the court and must have been well thought of by the late King Henry VIII. He was given the title of Earl of Hertford in 1537, Lord high Admiral in 1542, and was placed on the regency council of the young King Edward after the death of Henry.

As long as Rich supported Somerset he would find himself being rewarded, and for a time it worked. Although their religious views differed, they were happy to work alongside one another. Rich was happy to see Somerset's rise in power, though his support nearly endangered his own position, and he came close to being imprisoned in the Tower, and even losing his life.

By 1549, and most likely not helped by his brother's grasp for power, Edward Seymour's downfall had begun. Those around him in court felt he had become too powerful and needed to be got rid of. In October 1549 he was accused of having abused the power given to him by the council (many of whom had given it to him in the first place[24]). In King Edward's own words Somerset was guilty of his own 'ambition, vainglory, entering into rash wars in mine youth, negligent looking on Newhaven, enriching himself of my treasure, following his own opinion, and doing all by his own authority'. Somerset had seized the king and taken him from Hampton Court to Windsor, in the belief that whoever controlled the king would control the country, but he was wrong. Rich attended a council meeting at Mercers Hall on 7 October and was informed of what had happened.[25] A few days later a proclamation was issued to the City of London outlining the poor governance of Somerset. Fearing civil war, Somerset surrendered and was arrested for treason and imprisoned in the Tower.

Where was Rich in all of this? Well, we find him once more at the centre of it all, not as a key player but once more playing a supporting role in the key events. It would be Rich, as Lord Chancellor, who would produce the articles of treason which Somerset had been accused of. And it was Rich who went to the young king to inform him of Somerset's fate. And, of course, Rich's name can be found on the death warrant.

Somerset was not executed for treason on this occasion. He was released from the Tower and later restored onto the council in early 1550. However, this was not enough for him. He had tasted power and did not want to live without it, and so he began searching for supporters to back his claim for power and to remove the Duke of Warwick (John Dudley). Warwick, however, had already proved himself a suitable President of the Council, someone who was happy to guide the young king and not control him. He was considered trustworthy and not power hungry, and many supported him. A year later Somerset found himself arrested once more, this time for contemplating the Lord President's arrest and execution.[26] He was charged with attempting to force a change in government by trying to overthrow Dudley. Somerset was executed on 22 January 1552 on Tower Hill. Like many of his peers, who had risen as young men in the reign of King Henry VIII, Somerset had was ambitious for power, fame and fortune. Unfortunately, he also paid the price for his ambition.

Rich was quick to act, knowing how the tide was turning for Somerset. He switched to Dudley's faction, thus enabling his own survival. However, there were those around him who knew his true colours and had even accused him of betrayal. In order to ensure his survival he resigned his post as Lord

Chancellor in December 1551, and then removed himself from Court wide due to ill health and old age.

Whatever one's view of Rich, one thing that cannot be denied was his extensive knowledge of the law and his desire that it was followed.[27] An example of this can be seen a few months before he resigned as chancellor. In September 1551 an order was signed by the Privy Council ordering a commission for the examination of the Bishop of Worcester (Heath) and the Bishop of Chichester (Day), both of whom were vocal in their conservative religious views. The Privy Council had instructed Rich to seal the commission and to pass it to said commissioners for action. The problem Rich had with this was that there were only eight members in the Privy Council on that date. He sent it back to the Council, invalidating it due to there being an insufficient number of signatures.[28] Both Warwick and Edward VI wrote to Rich, frustrated at his refusal to do what was asked:

> I wrote a letter that I marvelled that he would refuse to sign that bill or deliver that letter that I had willed any one about me to write. Also, that it should be a great impediment for me to send to all my Council and I should seem to be in bondage. But by oversight it chanced and [not] thinking the more the better.[29]

Edwards letter is crossed out in the archives which could indicate the issue was resolved in some way. Warwick's and Rich's professional relationship was never one of great trust or friendship, and this certainly did not improve matters. Another reason that Rich may have been a stickler for the rules on this occasion was he could see it was within his power to try and assist fellow Catholics without bringing too much attention to his religious motives.

* * *

Plans were put into motion for Somerset's trial, and as Lord Chancellor, Rich had to create a commission and pass it under the Great Seal. He would have been happy to comply, not because he wanted to see Somerset dead but to try and show he was on the side of Warwick in an attempt to save his skin.[30]

Rich was expected to be present at Somerset's trial, on 1 December, but was not well enough to attend. It is said he used this as an excuse to keep away should attention be paid to him, and he is implicated in Somerset's downfall.

> Rich ought to have been created lord high steward to preside at the trial of the duke of Somerset; but he was not free from suspicion of being himself implicated in the conspiracy, and there was no knowing what disclosures might take place. He therefore feigned sickness [...] to give greater colour to the pretence, he issued a commission authorising the master of the rous and others to hear causes for him in chancery He shut himself up in his town-mansion, in Great St. Bartholomew's, and wrote to Northumberland that he was struck with a mortal disorder: that he was unable even to stir abroad to deliver up the great seal in person to the King, and praying that messengers might be sent to him to receive it, so that he might now devote all his thoughts to preparations for a better world.[31]

After Somerset was sentenced to death Rich, along with the rest of the council, sent him a letter 'to instruct him of suche thinges as might apperteign to the welthe of his sowle and to the patient taking of his worthie execution'. Somerset was executed on Tower Hill on 22 January 1552.

It is thought that Rich had secretly written to Somerset to inform him of the proceedings against him, maybe in an attempt to assist. However, in his haste he addressed the letter simply to 'the Duke' and gave it to a new servant to deliver. The servant, though, delivered it to Dudley instead.[32] On realising his grave error, Rich promptly went to the king the next morning and fell to his knees, 'and desired that his old age might be eased of his burthensome office; pleading that there ought to be some preparatory interval in statesmen betwixt their temporal business and their death, in order to which he desired to retire into Essex, there to attend his own devotions. Nor would he rise from the ground till the King had granted his request.'[33] Rich had managed to save himself through quick thinking and playing on his age, although he may have genuinely been too ill to attend.

What is known is that Rich certainly gave up the seal, most likely to save his own skin, knowing it was best to keep away from the Court. Dudley was not one to forget, and it would be Dudley and others who went to Rich's house to collect the Great Seal from him on 31 December 1551.[34] Retiring to his estates in Essex, Rich was made lieutenant for the county of Essex.[35] This retirement, coupled with his daughter Winifred's betrothal to Dudley's son Henry may have been the factors that enabled his survival and alowed him to escape punishment. Although Rich's role as Chancellor was a big part in Warwick's overthrow of Somerset (having the Great Seal on side to legitimise orders), he did not fully survive the coup intact. His loss of the chancellorship through Warwick's mistrust meant that Rich was never able to rise to such heights again.

* * *

England now had a 12-year-old boy king, assisted by John Dudley, Duke of Warwick, President of the Council (he chose not to take the title Lord Protector, which Somerset had used. Born c.1504, Dudley, son of Edmund Dudley, the ill-fated minister who was executed at the start of Henry VIII's reign, was considered one of the ablest and also most unprincipled party leaders to have turned to their advantage the resources and wealth of their country, 'few men have exhibited a great skill in intrigue, or a smaller regard for principle.'[36] A man who had experience on the battlefield and as a politician in court, he had witnessed the wrongdoings of Somerset. He had also seen the power he wielded and was shrewd enough not to overstep his mark. He knew it was best to work with the young king and offer guidance while letting Edward feel he was making the decisions in the ruling of England. Dudley was keen to be seen as acting on the king's behalf rather than to his own agenda.

After the downfall of Somerset, Dudley was created the Duke of Northumberland in October 1551. He was not a religiously motivated man, focused more on securing himself a position and surrounding himself with like-minded people.[37] Rich may have been viewed as one of those, for although a catholic at heart, he put his own goals above religion belief (as we have seen). Perhaps Dudley saw this in Rich and knew he was a man who could be useful. On assuming this power, Dudley had purged the council, in May 1552, of those he viewed as Catholic conservatives, though Rich and Cuthbert Tunstall, both of the Catholic faith, remained. Dudley knew the sense in keeping men who were good at their job even if they had political differences. There was no ignoring Rich's involvement in the torture of Anne Askew, especially for Dudley whose wife was a friend of Askew. Dudley and William Parr had even tried to persuade her to recant, but Dudley was able to put this to one side in order to work with him. Rich, too, was able to put aside his views on the new religion in order to wield some form of power. He accommodated himself to the new order and kept his office[38] under Warwick's leadership.

Under Dudley the young king was encouraged to be more involved in the running of the country. Dudley wanted mould him into the king he felt Edward should be, and by giving the teenager more control he was perhaps hoping he would keep Dudley by his side. From the age of about 14 Edward's signature on documents no longer needed the Council's countersignatures, and the king was regularly debriefed in meetings with a Council of his own choosing.[39]

* * *

Things continued as they were for a short time, with Rich withdrawing from the centre of Court. However, things were about to change. Edward started to show signs of being ill in January 1553 and by May Dudley realised the young king was dying, most likely of tuberculosis.

The Device for the Succession was Edward's version of the Act of Succession, but this was never passed in parliament due to time restraints as a result of his illness. Edward did not want his Catholic sister Mary taking the throne after his death, though this was the law as passed by his father in the 1543 act. If Edward excluded Mary, then he would have to exclude his other sister, Elizabeth. Edward wanted to create a new dynasty, 'one founded upon the true faith',[40] and decided, initially, for the throne to pass to his Aunt Frances', the Duchess of Suffolk's, male heirs. Frances was past childbearing age so the sons of her daughter, Lady Jane Grey, would inherit the throne, when she produced them. Edward's amended version stated that the throne would pass, 'To the Lady Franceses heirs males, if she have any such issue before my death to the Lady Jane and her heirs males.'[41] As this amended version was never passed in parliament it was technically illegal, but it was accepted by Edward's councillors as they had been left with little choice. Edward demanded their obedience, and 'on 21st June ordered his council to sign the new device […] many […] found their loyalties were torn […] many […] signed the device [with a troubled conscience].'[42]

Letters were sent to various councillors, including Rich, requesting their signature[43] in order to follow the king's wishes, and to keep the country Protestant. They were reluctant to sign it as it defied the Act of Succession, but, on the other hand, refusing the young king could be considered an act of treason, risking arrest and imprisonment. After some bullying by Dudley, the king's lords and councillors[44] put their name to the document, titled 'Engagement of the Council and others to maintain the Succession as limited by the King'.[45]

> the king's earnest desire and expressed commandment touching the limitation of the succession in the imperial crowne given us, agree, and by these presents signed with our hands and sealed with our seals, promise by our oaths and honours to observe, fully performed, and keep all and every article, clause, branche, and matter contained in the said writing [...] And we do further promise never to vary or swarve, during our lives, from the said limitation of the succession: butt the same shall to the utter most of our powers defend and maintain. And if any of us, or any other, shall at any time hereafter (which God forbid) vary from this agreement or any part thereof, wee and every of us doo assent to take, use, and repute him for a breaker of the common concord, peace, and unite of this realm [...] swarving, punished with most sharpe punishment, according to their desserts.[46]

Historians debate who was the original creator of Edward's Device for the Succession. Some believe it was all Edward's doing, while others state that Dudley was manipulating the king. Whoever was the mastermind, the Device set in motion events that placed not only Rich, but many others involved in court life at risk of facing charges of treason.

King Edward VI died on 6 July 1553. Dudley knew that many people would presume Henry VIII's Act of Succession would be followed, and so sent his son, Robert, to Hertfordshire to secure Mary[47] before she realised what was happening. But she had pre-empted his actions and had already secured herself to Kenninghall Palace, Norfolk, where she had a large support base, knowing her brother would not live long.[48] She began to gather support for her claim, knowing it was her right to become queen on Edward's death, and, on 8 July, sent a letter to the Council stating such and declaring herself queen:

> […] concerning the Crown and governance of this Realm of England […] what has been provided by act of Parliament and the testament and last will of our death father – beside other circumstances advancing our right – the Realm know and all the world knoweth […] Trusting also assuredly you will take and accept this grace and virtue in such good part as appeareth, and that we shall not be enforced to use the service of other our true subjects and friends which in this our just and rightful cause God, in whom our final affiance is, shall send us […] Wherefore, my lords, we require you and charge you, for that our allegiance which you owe to God and us, that, for your honour and the surety of your persons, you employ your selves and forthwith upon receipt hereof cause our right and title to the Crown and government of this realm to be proclaimed in our City of London and such other places […] And this letter signed with our hand shall be your sufficient warrant.[49]

The letter was ignored, but things did not go to plan for Dudley. Firstly, Jane did not wish to accept the Crown. Even she, as a Protestant, understood Henry's Act of Succession, and needed some persuasion before Dudley had her proclaimed queen on 10 July. Secondly, Dudley had also not envisioned Mary's quick thinking in amassing support and an army. Furthermore, she had relocated from Kenninghall to Framlingham, which was more secure. And thirdly, he did not realise the lack of support and reluctance of the majority of the councillors in court. Some had already shown their support for Mary and joined her at Framlingham. At this time, Rich still remained, openly at least, in support of Jane. He received a letter from the Council:

> After our right hartie commendations to you […] Although the matter contained in your letters of the Earl of Oxford's departing to the Lady Mary be grievous unto us for divers respects yet we must needs give our hearty thanks for your redi advertisement thereof Requiring your help nevertheless like a noble man to remain in that promise and steadfastness to our sovereign Lady Queen Jane's vice as ye shall find us redi and firm with all our force to the same Which neither with honor nor with saftie nor yet with duty we may now forsake.
>
> From the Tower of London, the 19th of July 1553.
>
> Your assured loving friends[50]

It seems that Rich had made them aware of Oxford's loyalty to Mary. For now at least he was trying to stay on the side that held the most power.

Three days later he received the Honour of Rayleigh, which was a reward for his information.

Dudley wanted to stay in London to keep a grip on things, but he also needed to put Mary in custody. It became apparent he was the only man experienced enough and willing to do the job and so he reluctantly left the capital and made his way to Suffolk, leaving the new queen with her father, the Duke of Suffolk. However, there was unrest amongst the councillors, for although they had declared for her, they all knew she was not the legal queen. King Henry had not been long gone, and they were still loyal to his wishes. Arundel, a keen supporter of Mary and William Herbert, Earl of Pembroke, arranged a meeting at Baynard's Castle to discuss the succession crisis, where a majority of councillors agreed that Mary was the rightful queen. On 20 July they issued a proclamation, declaring Mary as queen:

> In the year 1553 the 19th of July, the Counsell partlie moved with the right of the Lady Maries cause, partly considering that the most of the Realme was wholly bent on her side, changing their mind from Lady Jane lately proclaimed Queene, assembled themselves at this Baynard's Castle, where they communed with the Earle of Pembrooke and the Earle of Shrewsbury and Sir John Mason Clearke of the Counsell, sent for the Lord Mayor, and then riding into Cheape to the Crosse, where Gartar King at Armes, Trumpet being sounded, proclaimed the Lady Mary Daughter to king Henry the eight, and Queene Katharen Queene of England.[51]

Rich would have been happy to see this. Like others, he had started to make advances towards Mary, requesting her forgiveness and offering his services to her. This was not only so he could serve a Catholic monarch, but also to make sure he survived, which was his top priority.

Summons were issued from the Council to Northumberland to cease his activities and disband his army. He complied with this order, and, in Cambridge marketplace, declared for Mary through tears of grief. The following morning, he was arrested by Arundel, who had ridden to Framlingham after issuing the letter declaring the Council for Mary. It was she who sent him to arrest Northumberland, a man who declared he would spend his blood[52] (risk his life) for Northumberland before the duke left to take custody of Mary.

Northumberland was tried on 18 August at Westminster Hall and found guilty by his former colleagues and those he once considered his friends. After the sentence was passed, he pleaded to the queen to spare his sons. While awaiting his execution he even converted to the Catholic faith, most likely to try and secure his sons' survival rather than to save his own life or through a change in religious convictions. Northumberland was never really seen or considered a religious man at heart.[53] He had served in King Henry VIII's court and risen in power through his own abilities, and had built a strong base at Alnwick Castle. He was described by historian David Loades as self-interested but loyal to the monarch,[54] a description that could have been used for Rich, but unlike Rich, Northumberland misjudged the turning of the tide, leaving him in an impossible situation.

* * *

Under Edward, Rich had thrived even more than he had under Henry. He rose to one of the highest positions possible in the Tudor Court, procured more land, and established himself in Essex as a man of considerable standing. He did what was asked of him under a Protestant king, even at the cost of those he may have considered friends. He had managed to keep in with the Protestant gentry, even though they probably knew at heart that he was a Catholic. They clearly understood that he was useful, and though they may not have liked him, they needed him. Rich in turn knew that as long as he followed the king's wishes he would continue to prosper. He did not turn against Jane as his queen, despite knowing that she was not the legal monarch, thus continuing a pattern of behaviour – betrayal of friendships, enriching himself, and doing what he felt was necessary to survive – which enabled his progression under a new monarch.

England was once more a Catholic country, under the first Queen Regnant (a queen in her own right and not through marriage to the king). She had an unhappy upbringing. Her father, Henry VIII, turned his back on her and did not allowed her to see her mother, Catherine of Aragon, even when she was dying. And so she turned to religion, and her mother's home country of Spain, for support.

After years of religious upheaval, England was a divided country, with people on both sides of the religious divide who were not going to change their beliefs.

Religion and Richard Rich

The reign of King Henry VIII brought religious turmoil to the country. He broke with the Catholic church, renounced the authority of the Pope, and made himself head of the new Church or England. At the same time, the new Reformist religion, which would eventually be seen as Protestantism, was becoming more established in England. But though we may label people as either Catholic or Protestant during the Tudor era, it was not always so clear. Religion is a very personal matter, and it is not easy to judge one's actions based on their faith alone.

As for Rich, once Queen Mary knew she was victorious, she sent him, along with Oxford and their companions, to Ipswich to await further instructions.[1] Afterwards, at the beginning of August, she stayed as a guest at Rich's home in Wansted. He would certainly have used this opportunity to convince her of his loyalty and service. What made this visit more significant, was that Mary and her sister Elizabeth had united to denounce Jane Grey as queen. There were not many things that Henry's two daughters agreed upon but they both accepted their father's Act of Succession.

The next time we hear of Rich is when he is present at the Queen's Council on 12 and 13 August 1553,[2] and again the following month on 14 September. It was at September's meeting where Cranmer, another survivor of Henry VIII, was sent to the Tower of London for committing treason.

> This present daye, Thomas, Archbishop of Canterbury, appearing before the Lordes after long and serious debating of his offence by the whole Borde, it was thought convenient that as well for the treason committed by him against the Queens Heighnes, as for the aggravating of the same his offence by spreading abroad seditious bills moving tumultes to the disquietnes of the present state, he should be committed to the Tower, there to remain and be referred to justice, or further ordered as shall stande with the Quenes pleasure.[3]

Cranmer's trial commenced on 13 November 1554, the outcome being that he was found guilty and condemned to death. A second trial for heresy was held on 12 September 1555, this time under papal jurisdiction, where permission was given to proceed against him. Cranmer was burnt at the stake on 21 March 1556. A few days previously he had recanted and reverted back to the Catholic church. However just before being taken to Broad Street, Oxford (he had been imprisoned at Bocardo Prison, Oxford, since 8 March 1554), to meet his fate, he renounced his recantation and refused the Pope, calling him an Antichrist. Once tied to the stake, he placed the 'unworthy hand' that signed the presentation into the fire, 'which he held so steadfast and immovable'.[4]

* * *

In order to survive in the Tudor period, people had to adapt to the changes in how they worshipped depending on what the monarch had dictated, and most changed their religion in order to obediently follow their king.[5] He was their lord and sovereign and so it was their duty to do so. Some like More and Askew refused and became martyrs, putting their faith before their duty to Henry, while Northumberland and Cranmer both recanted in the hope of saving their souls or their family members. But what of Rich?

In following the orders of Henry VIII Rich had alienated himself from both the Catholics, due to his involvement in More's execution, and the Reformists for his part in the torture of Askew. Some could say he was no Catholic at all, not only for his part in More's execution but also his position as Chancellor of the Court of Augmentations and his part in the Dissolution of the Monasteries, not to mention that while Chancellor he collected evidence against the bishops who refused the first Book of Common Prayer in 1549. His part in More's downfall was not so much a betrayal of the Catholic faith as an attack on More as a person while carrying out the king's instruction. Many Catholics, or those who were religiously conservative, also agreed to denounce the Pope so that particular argument can be ignored when examining Rich's religious beliefs. Rich was a survivor, someone who was able to put his conscience aside in order to please the king and for self-advancement. However, Rich was a Catholic at heart and this is evident in the latter part of his life.

Rich's actions under Queen Mary I highlight where his religious preferences lay. From 1552 he was one of the most ardent persecutors of those who were considered heretics under Mary, who was deeply devoted to the core elements of the Catholic faith.[6] She has gone down in history as 'Bloody Mary' for her persecution of the many Reformists who were burnt at the stake on her orders.

As previously mentioned, Mary was not raised to become the ruler of a country. The years where she should have had some kind of training for being a head of state were instead filled with turmoil and isolation. When she was pronounced Queen of England, therefore, she lacked experience in ruling a country. Those she considered loyal to her cause would also have been kept at bay from making important decisions under her brothers reign due to his distrust of them. So, not only was she inexperienced, so too were those ministers close to her. She needed experienced men to help her, which was why men like Rich, who had seemingly betrayed her, were placed in positions of power.

Rich would be appointed a commissioner of claims for the queen's coronation, 'for the hearing and ordering of all such as shall make any claims for offices at the Coronation before the same Coronation.'[7] Others appointed with him were the Earl of Bath,[8] the Lord Paget and the Chief Justice of the Common Place.[9] Rich, to his relief, was also appointed as one of Mary's Privy Councillors. Unlike Henry's and Edward's reigns, Rich's attendance at Council meetings was infrequent under Mary. This could be due to his health, but also because he wanted to keep himself out of the limelight, or because Mary's advisors wanted him kept at bay.

After the execution of The Duke of Northumberland, Mary sent Rich to Syon house 'to collect into their hands to her Graces use all the goodes of the late attainted personnes, to repaire owt of hande to Syon, and to get into their handes the late Duke's goodes there, and to discharge awaye their servants,'[10] much as he had done with Catherine of Aragon. On 5 September he received another letter from the council, 'requiring them in the Queens Highness' name to forbear to make further sale of the said goodes till further of the Queens pleasour be known upon a sight of the inventarie of thole, because the Queen hathe granted certain stuff to the Lady Marques of Executor and to the Earl of Devon, her sonne.'[11] Whether Mary trusted Rich or not, she valued his experience.

The Catholic faith was restored to England once more. As previously stated, Rich had always being a Catholic at heart: he had founded Felsted Chantry at Felsted Church near his estate in Leighs;[12] he assisted the queen in restoring some of the monasteries; and he gave his townhouse of St Bartholomew's to the queen in September 1555,[13] in which she restored Blackfriars monastery. He also surrendered other properties (in 1558), including Rayleigh, and in recompense he was made steward of the manor.[14] It was around this time that Mary was reviving some of the closed monasteries and nunneries, including Syon, where it is thought Rich's youngest daughter, Barbara, entered the abbey as a nun.[15]

Although most people accepted Mary as their rightful queen, there were those who could not. These people had three choices: accept the Catholic religion and convert; go into exile; or face punishment,[16] which for most resulted in death. It would be Rich's responsibility to enforce punishment on those who chose not to convert.

> *29 January 1554*
> To Rich, the earl of oxford and others, just of Essex to the council. Measures for the safeguard and quiet of those parts and stay of the passages.[17]

> *19 February 1554*
> A letter to lord rich and sir john Wentworth knight, sheriff of Essex, for the punishment of certain lewd persons in Colchester, copshall and other places thereabouts, that have gone about to dissuade the queen's people there from frequenting such divine service as it presently appointed by the laws to be observed in the realm.[18]

It was around this time that Mary was looking to find a husband, and it would not have come as a surprise to many to discover her proposed suit was King Philip II of Spain, who was also her cousin.[19] However, there were many who were not happy with this arrangement, fearing that England would be drawn into Spain's wars. But Mary's mind was made up, and even though parliament tried to dissuade her, they eventually had to accept her choice. A few opponents decided that more drastic action would need to be taken, and a coup was set in motion to overthrow Mary and place Elizabeth on the throne.[20] In anticipation of possible unrest, Mary and her advisors tried to take action. When the articles of the marriage were made public, instructions were sent to the justices in the counties, including Rich, to suppress any attempts at rebellion,[21] and to take measures for the safeguarding of the counties.[22] Rich had written to Mary offering the services of Charles Tyrell and Robert Cornwall, even offering to supply them with armour.[23] The rebellion failed, and, due to her father's involvement in the uprising, Jane Grey was executed on 12 February 1554. The marriage of Mary and Phillip went ahead on 20 July at Winchester Cathedral.

* * *

At the sitting of the third parliament in November[24] England was officially reunited with Rome, along with the repeal of the Act of Supremacy. The Pope had agreed that the monastic lands could remain with those who had acquired them during the dissolution, not because it was their legal right but as a gift from the church to the laymen. The return of the monastic land to the church was something that worried Rich and other members of the Council who had spent money building their country estates from these former religious institutions, and the Vatican knew it was best to keep these men onside. Mary, however, was not satisfied with this. Rich felt certain he would not be compensated for any loss of property should he be forced to give back any former religious land either. He made a formal protest against the restoration of the Great Bishop of Durham feeling it would be the start of the former monastic land being handed back. When the bill (to restore the Great Bishopric) was sent to the House of Commons it was initially rejected but the former Bishop of Durham, Cuthbert Tunstall went to the House and pleaded his case, winning round enough to get the bill passed and the diocese of Durham was restored[25]. The House of Lords also rejected Mary's attempt at reviving the medieval heresy laws, and she chose not to push the restoration of former religious land back under the Catholic Church.

In the same parliamentary session, another bill was put through both Houses, to extend the treason laws to include Phillip of Spain. Rich, Arundel,

Shrewsbury, Paget and the bishops of London and Worcester were given the bill to review, and it was passed on 24 April, though changed from the one Mary wanted passed. It was only considered treason if one physically took up arms against Phillip rather than just talking about it. Mary was frustrated with the parliament, and with her councillors, who were led by Paget in opposition to Gardiner. Paget later explained that his opposition to some of the bills was because he had been convinced by Rich that the real purpose was to take back control of the monastic lands. Rich was clearly worried about the loss of his lands and would not have been alone in this, hence the support for him. He and Paget were not opposed to the marriage, but they wanted to show Mary that they held power and influence.

As with Henry VIII, Cromwell, Somerset and Northumberland, Rich served Mary to the best of his abilities (other than when his own status and wealth were put at risk). Any ill- will felt by Mary towards Rich was soon forgotten, and h became a member of her inner circle of advisors.[26] In his position as Justice of the Peace, he was responsible for prosecuting Protestant heretics in Essex. He carried out his task with great enthusiasm and was even congratulated by the Privy Council[27] for his efforts. He was assisted in his role by the Earl of Oxford along with another Essex gentry.[28] We know that on 18 March 1554 they were requested by the Council to be present at the burnings of 'such obstinate persons'.[29] The following year, on 3 June, Rich received a letter requesting him to be present at burnings in Colchester, Manningtree and Hardwicke,[30] and that any duties he had been previously requested to do by the Council were excused at this time.[31]

Initially it was thought the burning of a few heretics would encourage others to convert and abide by the restored Catholic faith, but the early burnings in February 1555 actually had the opposite effect. People in Cambridgeshire, where the early burnings took place, admired those who lost their lives. This made the Council proceed with more fervour, which in turn made some areas more volatile. Indeed, it was only the presence of Rich, Oxford and armed retainers in Essex that prevented potential riots.[32]

In June 1555 a man named Thomas Watts, who was about to be burnt at Chelmsford for heresy, spoke out against Rich, rebuking him and saying 'My Lord, beware, beware! For you do against your own conscience herein, and without you repent, the Lord will revenge it.'[33] He remembered Rich from

Somerset's time when he had held supposedly Protestant views (though, as we know, he was merely following orders). Watts was a line draper from Billericay, Essex, who refused to say Mass when it was reinstated by Queen Mary. He was arrested as a heretic on 5 February. In *Foxe's Book of Martyrs* it is said he was expected to be 'taken by God's adversaries'.[34] He was accused by Rich and others in Chelmsford of not going to church. He was questioned by Sir Anthony Browne, who asked him why he had embraced his heretical views, to which he replied that Browne himself had told him: 'in King Edward's days in open sessions you said the mass was abominable trumpery, earnestly exhorting that none should believe therein, but that our belief should be only in Christ.'[35] Foxe's account also states that Watts had also spoken against Queen Mary's husband, Philip of Spain, which was also considered treason. He was then sent to Bishop Bonner, who had earned the nickname 'Bloody Bonner' due to the number of burnings in his diocese of London and Essex. It is noted Bonner actually made several attempts to get Watts to convert before handing him back to the secular arm of the law (the Church was not legally allowed to take a life) and condemning him to be burnt at the stake.

Rich and his magistrates in Essex were keen to get Watts out of Essex before he caused them any further embarrassment:

> What basis there was for this claim is impossible to say. Browne, who, even in Elizabeth's reign, would remain a conservative catholic, vigorously denied it, declaring to Lord Rich, chairman of the bench, that Wattes had "belied" him. Rich tersely replied, "I dare say he does".[36]

Watts' conversion to the Protestant religion was carried out by a number of the clergy who were based in Essex during the reign of Edward VI, and who most likely owed their position to Rich's patronage. Rich was trying to recover from Somerset's fall and trying to get in Mary's good graces, and certainly did not want a reminder of his past deeds. Watts was sent back to The Lion Inn in Chelmsford until his execution on 10 June 1555. He was burnt along with Thomas Hawkes.

Other heretics/martyrs condemned by Rich included:

Nicholas Chamberlain, weaver, Coggeshall, executed in Colchester on 15 June 1555

Thomas Causton,[37] Horndon on the Hill/Thundersly, executed in Rayleigh 26 March 1555

John Ardeley, husbandman, Wigborough, executed in Rayleigh, 26 March 1555

Stephen Knight, barber, executed in Maldon 28 March 1555

William Pigott, butcher, burned at Braintree, 28 March 1555 John Simpson, husbandman, Wigborough, burnt 30 May 1555 (or 'about 10 June', according to Foxe) in Rochford

John Lawerence, priest, Sudbury, burnt 29 March, in Colchester

Colchester Martyrs, all burnt 28 April 1556, in Colchester:

Christopher Lister, husbandman

John Mace, apothecary

John Spencer, weaver

Simon Joyne, sawyer

Richard Nichols, weaver

John Hamond, tanner

There was a lot of 'heretical' activity around Rochford during this time, which may have been why Rochford and Rayleigh were the sites of some of the burnings. Rich, owning and sometimes residing in Rochford Hall, would most certainly have been a known figure in the area and expected to attend these burnings. After 1556 the majority of the burnings in Essex were done in Colchester.

On 18 December 1558, Rich was present at another burning. The man was John Philpot, son of a knight who had studied the civil law in his youth, who was 'zealous in religion, fearless in disposition'. He was archdeacon of Winchester when Mary came to the throne, and was called to discuss his view of the Reformation, which he defended in front of Gardiner. Following questioning, he was sent to Bonner to be questioned further, 18 months later, on 2 October 1555.

In his sixth examination Philpot was questioned by Rich and others, including the Lord St John. Philpot managed to write down most of his examinations and get them smuggled out, so it is interesting to see Rich's form of questioning when interrogating a 'heretic'.

[The following are extracts of Rich's questions and Philpot's responses. There were others present and involved. For the full transcript see Foxe's Book of Martyrs, *chapter 326]*

Rich: "How say you? will you acknowledge the real presence of the body and blood of Christ, as all learned men of this realm do, in the mass, and as I do, and will believe as long as I live, I do protest it."

Philpot: "My lords, that at first, I have not plainly declared my judgment unto you, the reason is this, because I cannot speak hereof without the danger of my life."

Rich: "There is none of us here that seeketh thy life or means to take any advantage of that thou shalt speak."

Philpot: "Although I mistrust not your honourable lordships that be here of the temporality; yet here is one that sitteth against me that will lay it to my charge even to death."

Rich: "My lord, permit him to say what he can, seeing he is willing to shew his mind."

Bonner: "I am content, my lords, let him say what he can, I will hear him."

Rich: "All heretics do boast of the Spirit of God, and everyone would have a church by himself; as Joan of Kent, and the Anabaptists. I had myself Joan of Kent a week in my house after the writ was out for her to be burnt, where my lord of Canterbury, and bishop Ridley resorted almost daily unto her: but she was so high in the Spirit, that they could do nothing with her for all their learning. But she went wilfully into the fire, was burnt, and so do you now."

Philpot: "As for Joan of Kent, she was a vein woman (I knew her well) and a heretic indeed, well worthy to be burnt, because she stood against one of the manifest articles of our faith, contrary to the scriptures."

Rich: "What countryman are you? Are you of the Philpots of Hampshire?"

Philpot: "Yea, my lord, I am sir P. Philpot's son, of Hampshire."

Rich: "He is my kinsman; wherefore I am the more sorry for him."

Philpot: "I thank your lordship that it pleaseth you to challenge kindred of a poor prisoner. In faith I would go an hundred miles on my bare feet to do you good."

Rich: "Well, I take your meaning: what if means be made to the queen's majesty that you shall have your request, will you be judged by them?"

Philpot: "My lord, it is not meet that a man should be judged by his adversaries."

Rich: "By whom then would you be judged?"

Philpot: "I will make your honours judges, that shall be hearers of us."

Rich: "I dare be bold to procure for you of the queen's majesty that you shall have ten learned men to reason with you, and twenty or forty of the nobility to hear, so you will promise to abide their judgment. How say you, will you promise here before my lords so to do?"

Philpot: "I will be contented to be judged by them."

Rich: "Yea, but will you promise to agree to their judgment?"

Philpot: "I will ask of my lord Rich here, whom I know to have good knowledge in the laws and statutes of this realm, although a judge may discern the meaning of a statute agreeable to the words, whether the same may judge a meaning contrary to the express words or no?"

Rich: "My lord of London, I pray you let Dr. Chedsey reason with him, and let us see how he can answer him, for I tell thee he is a learned man indeed, and one that I do credit before a great many of you, whose doctrine the queen's majesty and the whole realm doth well allow, therefore hear him."

Rich's questioning of Philpot shows, on the surface at least, that he was willing to hear all that Philpot had to say, and that he was rational in his response. He tried to give him a fair hearing and encouraged Philpot to be honest in his response. Philpot in turn also states that Rich is known for his knowledge of the law.

Philpot would undergo 14 examinations while prisoner, and was placed in the stocks for a time. It would be at his fourteenth examination that he was given his sentence, to be condemned as a heretic and taken to Newgate to await execution the following day. The next morning, at about eight o'clock, he met the sheriffs and was taken out and burnt. In the aftermath of these burnings, around 80 men and women in total, both Rich and Oxford received letters of thanks for 'pains taken in assisting the shire of Essex in executing certain persons'.[38]

* * *

Rich was acting as a royal agent, and was critical in making sure that instructions on church attendance were followed. As a result, Rich is painted as the villain for his role in the burning of heretics at this time. I am not going to defend him for his part in this, but it must be stated that there is one other person who was carrying out the same role and who needs a brief mention. The man's name was Edmund Tyrell. Born c.1513, he was a JP in Essex at the time of Mary's reign, and was from a cadet branch of one of the oldest and best-known families in Essex at the time. He leased the rectory of Hockley in 1536 for 21 years and renewed it further.[39] He was fierce in his attack towards heretics in Essex, and this 'brutal efficiency' brought him to the attention of Queen Mary and Phillip.[40] Tyrell was not shy of hunting down heretics or reporting them. One report which shows Tyrell's harshness regards the questioning of a woman called Rose Allin. Her parents were known to Tyrell as being heretics, and as a JP for the area, Tyrell had been watching their house. On advising her of her parents' heretical ways, she replied that they had better instruction in religion than he had and what he called heresy she regarded as God's truth. Angered by her response, Tyrell grabbed her hand and held it to the flame of a candle until it burned out. She did not cry out or fight while undergoing this ordeal, which seemed to infuriate Tyrell even more. Foxe described Tyrell as having either a blind zeal or parasitic flattery, '[the] hammer of the heretics in Essex. His survival in the reign of Elizabeth after such a zealous attack of Protestants was most likely down to his friendship and Patronage with William Petre and William Parr. His only "punishment" was the loss of his seat on the Essex bench.'[41]

* * *

It was not just heretics in England whom Rich had been tasked with persecuting. As previously mentioned, on the ascension of Mary some chose to flee abroad. Some members of the upper ranks who fled from persecution were Sir Peter Carew, William Cecil, Sir John Cheek and Sir Thomas Wroth. In 1556 Rich was on the commission to investigate those who had fled England on religious grounds.[42] In February he was requested by the Council to stop a supposed heretical play at Hatfield Broad Oak, Uttersford, Essex. He was further instructed to examine the players, the effect the play may have had, and to make sure no one was able to see the play.[43]

Aside from persecuting heretics, Rich was tasked with setting an example on how to behave and worship like other people of standing in Essex. On Sunday, 20 August, Rich and others of the Queen's Council, such as the Lord Treasurer, the Earl of Bedford, and Lord Wentworth, were appointed to be present at the sermon of Mr Watson, a Bachelor of Divinity and Chaplain to the Bishop of Winchester, at Pawleys Crosse. Worried about a possible uprising, there guards present at the pulpit, with a warning issued by the Lord Mayor to all companies of the city to be present and to wear their liveries for all to see.

* * *

In 1558 England had joined Spain once more in their dispute with France. This had drastic consequences for Mary, something for which she was forever blamed, the loss of Calais. It had been under English rule since 1346, when it was conquered after the Battle of Crecy, led by King Edward III. It was a significant foothold in France, under English rule and strategically placed for defence and attack. The loss of English control, though not a major economic factor, was forever on Mary's mind. On her deathbed she is said to have uttered 'When I am dead and opened, you shall find "Calais" lying in my heart.'

* * *

In his personal life Rich founded the Rich Chantry in Felsted Church on 25 April 1555. A chantry was set up by those with wealth to pay for monks, nuns or priests to say masses for their souls in the hopes it would assist them in going to heaven when they died. It could be part of a church, an area secluded off, or in some cases a small chapel would be created alongside a church. Another reason for the creation of his chantry was the death of his eldest son, Hugh, the same year. Perhaps the grief of losing a child caused Rich to examine his soul. At the same time, he also created a herring dole charity for the poor of Felsted:

> And I do order that the said churchwardens for the time being shall take and receive the profits of such lands, tenements, parsonages and hereditaments… and therewith buy yearly for ever eleven barrels of white herrings and eleven barrels of red heroes…and distribute seven barrels of red herrings…to the poor householders of Felsted…where the most need shall be…one barrel of white herring and one…of red…to begin upon Ash Wednesday and so weekly every Sunday in the afternoon during Lent…till the seven barrels of…herrings be fully given and distributed.[44]

The other barrels were distributed between Great Waltham, and Little Leighs. After time, the dole turns into cash of £35 a year from governor Felsted school. It is the oldest charity still in existence at Felsted today.

* * *

Mary Tudor died on 17 November 1558. She did not have any children to inherit the throne, so, reluctantly, named her sister Elizabeth as her successor. Even though she wanted a Catholic to follow her, she knew Elizabeth was legally the next in line. Mary pleaded with her sister to not undo what she had done and to keep England Catholic.

Under Queen Mary, Rich was able to reveal his true beliefs. It may have been due to the fact that it was again safe to be Catholic, or it could have been the death of his eldest son, or simply entering the later years of his life, but Rich began to look after his spiritual self rather than just his possessions on earth. Although not at the centre of things, as he had been previously, he was still involved in the governance of England, more precisely in his own small kingdom in Essex. Perhaps the close call with Somerset had shown him how dangerous too much power could be. Rich was a survivor, and he wanted to die of natural causes rather than on the scaffold.

As for the prosecution of Protestants, one cannot be surprised to see him carrying this out with enthusiasm. After all, how many of his fellow Catholics had faced persecution and death in previous reigns, and probably believed he was doing God's work, not torturing people for the sheer enjoyment of it (one hopes). Rich survived his third Tudor monarch, but he would never reach the great heights of power again.

The Last Years of Richard Rich

By 1558, when Elizabeth, the last remaining Tudor, became Queen of England, Rich was entering old age. He was around 62 years old, and possibly beginning to tire of court politics and intrigue, choosing instead to stay at his main residence of Leighs Priory. On occasion he still played a role in politics, and though he had been involved in many dubious activities, he was still seen as an experienced elder member of the court.

He accompanied the new queen on her progress into London, and at the coronation he managed to get his son and heir, Robert, made a Knight of the Bath. Rich was not immediately appointed onto Elizabeth's new council, which may be an indication of her, or her Chief Advisor William Cecil's[1], lack of trust in him[2]. He was clearly missing the active life in the monarch's court as he wrote frequently to her, requesting an audience. His letters seemed to have done the trick as Elizabeth did call upon his services on numerous occasions. Rich would serve on a commission to enquire into the grants of land made under Mary.

In March 1558 a ship was wrecked on the Essex coast, near one of Rich's manors. Rather than send it to the queen and council, Rich initially claimed it for himself, perhaps believing that as it was on his land he therefore owned it. This was not the case, and Rich was ordered to surrender the ship on 9 July the same year.[3] It was around the same time that Rich acquired the manor of Hockley, near his estate of Rochford. He sent a letter to the queen asking her to sell it to him and in return she would have his heart's blood in her service. It was sold to him for 1066l 13*s* 4*d* (roughly £248,865.07 in today's money[4]). Rich was called upon to ensure that religious stability was maintained in his home county. In December 1558 he investigated a man named Thomas Pike, who disrupted services in Shoebury Magna.[5] He was instructed to punish him according to the severity of his offence.[6]

Rich was graced with the queen's presence at three of his estates during her progress in 1561.[7] Though this was a huge expense on his part, he must have been hugely proud of such an honour, and no doubt bragged about it.[8] When the monarch went on progress it was no small affair and there was a lot of organisation involved. Elizabeth had at least 20 coaches for her ladies and advisors, and 300 baggage carts, and she expected to be entertained. It is estimated he spent around £389, nearly double what Sir William Petre spent when she visited him at Ingatestone Hall. The other manor she visited was Wanstead, where she had previously stayed with Mary in August 1553.

In February 1563 Rich requested another audience with the queen to discuss an important manner, one that he was not alone in being concerned about: her marriage, the succession, and the security of the realm. It is not known what transpired at this meeting, but he was not banished from her court, so she was clearly not overly offended by his 'advice'. Three years later, Elizabeth was still not married,[9] and Rich joined a delegation of 60 members from both houses to address her on the subject once more. Many were growing concerned that she had still not married, eight years into her reign and 33 years of age. Elizabeth was not impressed, and issued a statement, which Cecil duly passed on:[10]

> I did send them an answer by my council, I would marry (although of my own disposition) but that was not accepted nor credited, although spoken by their Prince.
>
> I will never break the word of a prince spoken in a public place, for my honour's sake. And therefore, I say again, I will marry as soon as I can conveniently.
>
> The second point was for the limitation of the succession of the crown, wherein was nothing said for my safety, but only for themselves [...] though I be a woman, yet I have as good a courage answerable to my place as ever my father had. I am your anointed Queen. I will never be by violence constrained to do anything. I thank God I am indeed endowed with such qualities that if I were turned out of the realm in my petticoat, I were able to live in any place in Christendom.
>
> Your petition is to deal in the limitation of the succession. At this present it is not convenient, nor never shall be without some peril unto you, and certain danger unto me. But as soon as there may be a convenient time and that it may be done with least peril unto you, although never without great danger unto me, I will deal therein for your safety and offer it unto you as your prince and head without requests. For it is monstrous that the feet should direct the head.[11]

Although not holding an official title, Rich was allowed to style himself as a councillor until his death. Though no longer in close proximity the monarch, he would not lay idle. He was used to being a man of authority and put himself to use in Essex where his power base lay, through his numerous landholdings and position as a landlord. He kept himself busy, and was in parliamentary elections. In 1562 he tried, unsuccessfully, to get his son and heir, Robert Rich, made a Knight of the Shire (the council's preferred candidate was William Petre.[12])

During this time Rich managed to rebuild some of his property portfolio, which he had surrendered to Queen Mary and the Crown. These included his former townhouse of St Bartholomew's in London.[13]

* * *

Unlike her brother and sister, Elizabeth chose not to punish those who did not adopt the same religious beliefs as she did (to begin with anyway). No one would be punished for having persecuted Catholics under her brother's rule or for persecuting and torturing Protestants under her sister Mary's rule, which would have come as a relief to Rich. It was this declaration that most likely led to some Catholics supporting Elizabeth. As long as they were prepared to recognise her as rightful queen and serve her as they had done her brother, sister and her father, then they would be safe from harm.[14]

However, this did not mean that everyone would support everything Elizabeth wanted. Rich became more open in his Catholic beliefs and would be one of those to openly speak against Elizabeth's religious settlement in 1559. It was not the first time a monarch had changed how England and its people observed the word of God, but it was the first time on record of Rich being openly opposed to it. This was a man who had always followed the wishes of his monarch. Why did he decide to speak up now?

The Act of Uniformity, the first political act to be passed in 1559, dictated the new rules on religious services including the use of the prayer book. It also stated that anyone not attending church would be fined one shilling and could be labelled a recusant. Along with Rich, others opposed it, including the Earl of Shrewsbury, the Lord Treasurer, and other Catholic supporters. They felt Elizabeth was going too far. It seems that Rich, knowing he was in the winter of his life, was placing more focus on his religious faith rather than worrying about offending his monarch.

Rich did support Elizabeth's Act of Supremacy, passed in the same parliament, though this was purely for his own gain. The act required all clergy and government to swear to accept Elizabeth as Supreme Governor of the Church. Unlike Henry's Act of Supremacy, this new act labelled Elizabeth as governor rather than head in the hope of appeasing Catholics. It allowed them (behind closed doors, of course) to acknowledge the Pope as head of the Church.

> I… do utterly testify and declare in my conscience that the Queen's Highness is the only supreme governor of this realm, and of all other her Highness's dominions and countries, as well in all spiritual or ecclesiastical things or causes, as temporal, and that no foreign prince, person, prelate, state or potentate hath or ought to have any jurisdiction, power, superiority, pre-eminence or authority ecclesiastical or spiritual within this realm; and therefore I do utterly renounce and forsake all foreign jurisdictions, powers, superiorities and authorities, and do promise that from henceforth I shall bear faith and true allegiance to the Queen's Highness, her heirs and lawful successors, and to my power shall assist and defend all jurisdictions, pre-eminences, privileges and authorities granted or belonging to the Queen's Highness, her heirs or successors, or united or annexed to the imperial crown of this realm. So, help me God, and by the contents of this Book.[15]

By supporting the Act of Supremacy Rich was able to protect his earthly wealth, while opposing the Act of Uniformity protected his soul.[16]

One result of the religious changes under Elizabeth's reign was the closure of chantries. Rich had founded the Rich Chantry at Felsted Church under the reign of Queen Mary, and instead of losing the hard work and money that had been put into it, he had it transformed into a Felsted School for Boys, which is still in existence today, though on a new site. In the deed founding the school, Rich provided a schoolmaster and usher to run the school, as well as school housing and dwellings. He also installed a priest who would be chosen by Rich's heirs when he needed to be replaced. There were places for 80 boys, all of whom had to be born in Essex to be eligible for a place.

> Richard Lord Rich did, in the year 1564, found a Free school in Felsted, with good provision for a Schoolmaster and Usher, and appropriated to the use of the same, as follows:
>
> A good Schoolhouse standing just before the south-side of the Church, fronting the street: A good Dwelling house for the Master, with a garden and close adjoining, of about two acres, and other conveniences, standing upon the road leading from Felsted-Church towards. Stebbing or Braintree: A convenient Chamber adjoining to the School for the Usher.
>
> He ordered the Chaplain of the foundation to be a Priest, chosen by the heirs of the founder, named and collated in writing. The Chaplain to be a Schoolmaster, to teach eighty male children born in Essex. The Usher to teach the Children in such manner and form as the schoolmaster shall direct. Upon complaint of the Master to the heirs, the Usher is to be displaced, and another put in his room. The schoolmaster and Usher not to be absent above eight days in a quarter, without good excuse. If the Schoolmaster or Usher be removed, another to be put in within six weeks, or else the Bishop of London may collate. If the Chaplain or Schoolmaster have any spiritual promotion other than by the gift of the heirs, then to be removed. A Sermon to be preached on Whitsunday in the afternoon, and at the end thereof this Psalm.[17]

It is interesting for Rich to have founded a school. In 1541, Canterbury Cathedral ceased to be a Benedictine monastery but reverted to being a college of secular men, with a grammar school attached. Cranmer, Rich and others entered into a discussion on who should attend this school. Cranmer decided it should not just be for the elite upper members of society's children but for any child with the ability for education. At the time it was noted that a few of Cranmer's peers, including Rich, were surprised at this and felt education should be for gentlemen's sons only, as they were to 'have the knowledge of government and rule in the commonwealth'. Cranmer's reply, knowing that he and others, including Rich, were from a similar background, noted:

> poor man's children are many times induced with more singular gifts of nature, which are also the gifts of God, as with eloquence, memory, apt pronunciation, sobriety, with such like, and also commonly more given to apply their study than is the gentleman's son, delicately educated [...] The ploughman's son, it was argued, should follow the plough [...] there was as much need of ploughmen as of other classes [...] and all sorts of men may not go to school.[18]

Cranmer, although charitable in nature, had also worked closely with the upper ranks of society and knew full well that noble birth did not necessarily mean that people were equipped for the task of running the country, and was not afraid to voice these views. Maybe Rich heeded Cranmer's words and realised he could provide a good start for those in the lowest ranks of society. It could also be that he was looking once more to his mortal soul and trying to do good deeds to balance the bad ones before he met his maker.

In addition to the school, Rich would also establish an almshouse[19], on 23 December 1565, to house up to six people, with the money most likely coming from the income generated from Braintree rectory.[20]

> Lord Rich assigns very liberal maintenance for six alms folk one of whom is to be a woman capable of seeing the housekeeping ad doing the housework [...] each is to have a separate chamber and the use of a common hall (sitting room) with outhouses and cowhouses and pigsty and land for a kitchen garden [...] general control of the alms-houses and residents to be with chaplain and churchwardens [...] inmates to attend daily service and pray for the welfare of the Rich family.

* * *

In December 1558, Rich's wife, Elizabeth, died aged 48. Perhaps this was another reason for him to look to his soul in the afterlife. They had been married for around three decades and it seems to have been a happy marriage on the whole, with no written evidence of any discord between them. The only potential evidence of it not wholly being a love match was the birth and acknowledgement of Rich's bastard son, another Richard, who was born after Elizabeth and Rich had married. She was buried in Felsted Church. A record of her death and funeral was noted in Henry Machyn's Diary:[21]

> The 13th day of December was [buried] my lade Rich..., the wyff of the... lord Rich..., with a herse of 5 prynsepalles and a viij dosen penselles and a viij dosen skochyons and a grett baner of my lords and my ladies armes and iiij baner rolles, and iiii baner(s) of santtes; and brett wyatt branchys and vj

dosen of torchys; and xxiiij pore men had gowns; and the morrow masse and a greet denver, and in harolds and money mourners.[22]

* * *

On 12 June 1567 Rich died at Rochford Hall, most likely from natural causes. He was around 70 years old. His heir was his surviving son, Robert Rich. His will had been officially signed and witnessed on 12 May 1567. He appointed as his executors Sir Robert Catlin, Chief Justice of the Queen's Bench, Sir William Cordall, Master of the Rolls, Attorney General Gilbert Gerrard, and his steward, William Bourne. Aside from the latter, these were all men of very high standing in the legal world, an indication of Rich's own status.

* * *

The will of SIR RICHARD Rich knight, [FIRST] LORD Rich, 20 May 1567

SIR RICHARD Rich knight, [FIRST] LORD Rich, 20 May 1567 [11/12] To be buried in Felsted church, the order and manner of my burying and the charges I commit to the discretion of my executors. For my tithes negligently forgotten I bequeath to the vicar of Little Leighs 13s. 4d.

My executors principally shall cause my debts to be paid with as convenient speed as they may as well to our sovereign lady the Queen as to all other persons.

To Agnes Piggott, one of the daughters of my daughter [Margery wife of Henry] Pigott of Abington [Cambs.], 500 marks towards her marriage if she be not before married in my lifetime. To Lucy Barley, one of the daughters of my daughter [Dorothy widow of Francis] Barley [of Kimpton, Herts.], 200 marks likewise. To Dorothy Pigott, one of the daughters of my daughter [Anne wife of Thomas] Piggott of Stratton [in Biggleswade, Beds.], 500 marks likewise. To Anne Drury, one of the daughters of my daughter [Audrey widow of Robert] Drury [of Hawstead, Suffolk], 500 marks likewise. To Elizabeth Darcy, one of the daughters of my daughter [Frances wife of John Lord], 500 marks likewise. Which legacies to be paid at marriage, to be levied of my goods and chattels and revenues of my lands. If any die before marriage, her portion to the next younger sister; if any shall marry without the consent of her father and mother, her portion to the next sister. To such of my executors as shall specially travail for the advancement in marriage of any of the same by his industry and travail £20.

To Sir Robert Rich knight, my son and heir apparent, as much of my plate at his choice as shall be to the value of £200 and all my household stuff, being no silver or gold, at any houses of Leighs, Rochford and St Bartholomew, with my artilleries, guns, harness and munitions of war, and my great stoned horses.

To every of my gentlemen that be my servants at the time of my decease and not advanced to any farm or annuity £5, to every other menservants being my household servants not advanced 53*s.* 4*d.*, and to every of my women and maidservants not advanced on their marriages 40s. To Anne wife of Thomas Shaa gentleman £10 and to my servant John Richardes £10.

My executors shall dispose in alms to the poor people coming to my burial 100 marks and shall be reasonably allowed for their expenses, pains and travail. To William Bourne my servant £10, and in consideration of his service heretofore done and to be done to me and to my son, taking like wages of my son, an annuity of £5 out of my manor and lordship of Rochford. Every person that stand bound for me and for my debt to the late kings Henry VIII or Edward VI or to any other person shall be discharged of their bonds by my executors [out] of the revenues of my lands.

To Sir Robert Catlyn knight, Chief Justice of the Queen's Bench, Sir William Cordell knight, Master of the Rolls, Mr Gilbert Gerrard, General Attorney, and to the said William Bourne, each £40, all of whom I ordain my executors. To them the manors of Great Waltham, Braintree and Newarks in Good Easter with the four prebends and parsonage there, lands called Watermans in Great Waltham, that parcel of Abchild Park called Waltham Quarter as is divided from the residue of the park, the manors of Broomfield Hall, Chatham Hall [in Great Waltham], Passelowe Hall [in High Ongar], Shelley, Brendish [in Moreton], Fyfield, Herons [in Fyfield], Upper Hall and Nether Hall in Moreton, Greensted Hall, the hundreds of Ongar and Harlow, the manors of Wanstead with the late park, Hatfield Broad Oak alias King's Hatfield with the mill and late park of Hatfield, Hutton Hall, Breames [in Great Leighs], Moulsham Hall [in Great Leighs], Warrakes [in Little Leighs], and Felsted with Grandcourts barn, the tithe corn of Fery

Quarter in Felsted with the lands and pastures called Blakeley, the manors of Enviles [in Great Leighs], Glandviles and Whelpstones [both in Felsted], the messuages called Gales in Felsted and Frenches at Horne in Felsted, the Old Park near Pleshey, and the five pastures late parcel of the park, the manors of Leighs and Leighs Rich with the farms or messuages called Camsex, Slampesey and Ravyns, the yearly rent of £5 out of the manor of Lyon Hall in Little Leighs, the manors of Westwicke Hall and Estwicke [both in Burnham], my part of the manor of Barlande [in Prittlewell] and Blakes in Prittlewell, and my lands in the same manors and parishes (except the site and capital messuage house of my manor of Leighs with Little Leighs Park and Lytley Park and the Forest of Hatfield, such lands, parsonages and tithes as I shall have in my own occupation towards the provision of my house at the time of my decease, and provision of corn, grain and cattle); and also my fair of Great St Bartholomew with the profits; to hold the same for 6 years after my decease to the intent that they shall with the issues and profits perform my will.

To my son Sir Robert and his heirs male the site and capital mansion house of my manor of Leighs alias Leighs Rich with all houses thereto belonging, the parks of Leighs and Lytley and the Forest of Hatfield, my lands, parsonages and tithes that I keep in my hands in Leighs and Felsted for the provision of my house, corn, grain and cattle, and the manors and lands bequeathed to my executors, after the expiration of the same years; and for default of such issue the remainder to my heirs male. Whereas it hath pleased God besides divers sons to send me divers daughters, i.e. Margery Piggott my eldest daughter, wife of Henry Pygott of Abingdon esquire, Agnes Mordaunt my second daughter, wife of Edmund Mordaunt esquire, Dame Mary Wrothe my third daughter, wife of Sir Thomas Wrothe knight, Dorothy Barley my fourth daughter, late the wife of Francis Barley esquire, Anne Piggot my fifth daughter, late the wife of Thomas Pigott of Stratton esquire, Audrey Drury my sixth daughter, late the wife of Robert Drury esquire, Elizabeth Payton my seventh daughter, wife of Robert Payton esquire, Dame Winifred North my eighth daughter, wife of Sir Roger North knight, Lord North, and the Lady Frances Darcy my ninth daughter, wife of Lord John Darcy of Chiche; if I shall die without issue male, all the said manors shall remain to my several daughters and their heirs. [Mordaunt, of

Thunderley in Wimbish; Wrothe, of Enfield, Middx.; Peyton, of Isleham, Cambs.; North, of Kirtling, Cambs.]

To Sir Robert the manors of Hockley, Hadleigh, Prittlewell and Pryors Marshes, Earls Hall alias Earls Field in Prittlewell, Eastwood, Sutton Temple, Southchurch, South Shoebury, and Milton Hall [in Prittlewell], my parts of the manors of Butlers in Shopland and the manors, lands, rents, reversions and services which were lately of Sir Henry Cary knight, now Lord Hunsdon, in possession or in reversion, in the hundred of Rochford (except such of the said manors late of Lord Hunsdon hereafter otherwise appointed); and for default of heirs male, the remainder to my daughters and their heirs. To Sir Robert the manors of Rochford and Combes and the farms of Myntons, Strowdwicke and Swaynes, the mill of Rochford and the tilekiln, and the rents of the same; and for default of such issue, the successive remainders to me and my heirs male and to Richard Rich, my base son, and his heirs male; and for default, the remainder of the manors of Rochford and other the premises last before specified to Edward Rich of Horndon [on-the-Hill] and his heirs male. Also to Richard, my base son, and his heirs male my manor of Patching Hall otherwise Woodhall Wall with those lands called Le Hyde in Broomfield and Chelmsford belonging.

My executors [out] of the issues aforesaid shall provide or buy one woman ward or some other woman having manors and lands of value of £200 yearly for a marriage to Richard, and shall pay him at marriage £500; and if he refuse to marry her or if no marriage shall be provided they shall pay him £1,000 and sell the ward or other woman if any such be provided to any other person to the uttermost advantage to the performance of my will. Anthony Browne shall have his government and bringing up in godly education and learning in the common laws or otherwise and shall receive the issues of the manors given to Richard towards his finding, apparelling and bringing up to the age of 21; and if he die before Richard is 21, Sir Robert Catlyn shall have his bringing up, and if Sir Robert die, Sir William Cordell shall have it.

The residue of all my manors and lands I leave to Sir Robert, provided that, if he willingly and advisedly shall practise in any court spiritual or temporal anything to molest, hinder, deny, vex or trouble my executors, then I bequeath to Richard, my base son, the manors of Brendishe, Shelley, Passelowe, Herons and Fyfield and to his heirs male, on condition that, if he or his heirs male shall at any time hereafter sell or give them, my heirs shall enter into them notwithstanding, and the gift to be void. Witnesses: the Lady Elizabeth Rich, John Boswell notary public, William Turner, M.A., and Thomas Mayew, with others.

[Codicil, 10 June 1567]
To Edward Ellis, yeoman of my cellar, 53s. 4d. yearly for life out of my manor of Rochford on condition that he serve my son and heir in the same office justly, taking like wages as he now taketh of me. Whereas I have bequeathed the manors which lately were of Sir Henry Cary to Sir Robert, I bequeath out of them to the almshouse to be erected in Rochford 5 or 6 acres of wood, parcel of Strowdewicke, called Britchetley, other ground parcel thereof containing 3 or 4 acres, with Little Downes and Brickle Close, 5 acres in Rochford Park on the north side leading down where the vault shall go, a marsh called Wakeringes in Great Wakering in the occupation of Robert Edmondes, also as much ground within the clapgate leading to Rochford town as shall serve for the site, garden and orchard where the almshouse shall be builded as is now staked out. To John Planten my servant 40s. yearly out of my manor of Felsted for life…Proved 3 June 1568, Sir Robert Catlyn renouncing executorship.[23]

* * *

At the time of his death Rich had probably accumulated an annual income of around £2,000. He had become one of the most important men in Essex alongside the Earl of Oxford (John de Vere, who like Rich had acquired a large amount of land in Essex). It is also interesting that Rich had provided for the welfare of his illegitimate son Richard who was still considered a minor. Although Sir Anthony Browne died before Rich, so the young Rich's care was placed with Sir Roert Catlyn.[24]

After his death Rich's body was laid in state at Rochford hall for four weeks, hung with black drapes, before being transported to Leighs Priory, ready for his funeral which was to be held the following day at Felsted Church. His body was carried in a 'charyot' pulled by horses, dressed with 'scothins and shafrons of his arms', riding behind a number of knights and gentleman, all dressed in black and on horseback. The procession rested the night in Chelmsford, with the body being placed in the court hall, being moved to Leighs the following day. On the day of his funeral, 8 July, he was 'carried honourably' to Felsted Church where his funeral took place, with his son being chief mourner, along with six other mourners. His funeral arrangements would have been carried out by the College of Arms owing to his status.

A funeral of a member of the nobility in the 16th century was one of tradition and a public occasion rather than a solemn private one for the family. It was a ceremony which impacted the state as well as the family of the deceased. The monarch's officers of arms would attend, continuing the hierarchy and social order that was followed in life and continued even in death.[25]

* * *

Today, Rich lies beneath a canopied tomb, with a life-size statue of Rich in his prime as Lord Chancellor, in his robes and round cap. He is laying down with an elbow resting on a cushion while holding a book of prayers. Above the statue is a blank panel which was possibly meant to have had an inscription.

Standing to the east end of the tomb is a young Rich holding a book with two seals, accompanied by his dog. To his side stands a female, believed to be representing the cardinal virtues as she holds a mirror and serpent for trust. His time as Speaker for the House of Commons is illustrated in a carved panel to the left which shows a mace and sword and short robe, and behind stand two females, one depicting fortitude and the other justice (she bears the sword and scales). His role as Lord Chancellor can be seen in the panel to the right in a similar design. The purse of the great seal is in one hand. Also depicted in this panel are hope, charity, fortitude and justice. One of the black marble groups beneath the panels shows Rich lying in state with a male at his head and a female in prayer, and above is a winged figure depicting fame, indicating his high estate and noble charity. This tomb is customary for someone of Rich's standing. It was built after the death of his son, Robert, by Robert's son in 1619, and was designed by the sculptor Epiphanius Evesham. Robert had dictated in his will that his son was to build a tomb for his father and grandfather in the chancel of the parish church of Felsted, or in a chapel adjoining the church. 'In his own will he instructed the executors to erect within 18 months of his death, tombs for his father, grandfather, great grandfather and his uncle Richard.'[26]

* * *

Bernard Gers[27] states a person does not need to be moral in order to be happy and live a fulfilling life, which feels entirely suited to Richard Rich. He was a survivor of the Tudor court, prospering under four of the five Tudor monarchs. A man with a reputation for immorality, perjury and dishonesty, only once did he face the risk of imprisonment[28] due to his involvement with Somerset. He never faced serious threat to his life, nor did any member of his immediate family, and not many who served the Tudor court could say that. He left behind him an heir to inherit his titles and wealth and daughters who had all been married to reasonably wealthy men of good standing in the county of Essex. Rich may have begun to tire of court life and servitude, and his last years were spent in Essex overseeing his 60 estates, some of which are still around today. Although he established a school and a charity for the poor, this is often overlooked, outweighed by his reputation for greed and the betrayal of those who may have considered him a friend.

The Rich Family

Richard Rich's life was a successful one. He left the world with a large property portfolio and a large fortune, along with two surviving sons, one illegitimate but acknowledged, and nine daughters. His descendants would continue his legacy for the next three centuries, with his grandson, another Robert Rich, being created the first Earl of Warwick in 1618.[1]

Rich's daughters

All bar one of his daughters were be married into families of the minor gentry, some residing in Essex, close to their father and his seat of power. It was a common occurrence within gentry and nobility to marry children, especially daughters, to build links and loyalties. His daughters may have been placed in other noble households and educated, with maybe the additional hope of a marriage into the hosting family to extend on family ties and bonds of marriage.

Margaret, born c.1526 married Henry Pygot of Abington,[2] Cambridge sometime before 1565. They had one daughter, Agnes.

Agnes, born c.1527, married Edmond Mordant (d. 1592), son of William Mordant of Hempstead, Essex,[3] sometime between c.1540 and 1544. They had six children. It is thought an Edmund Mordant attended Middle Temple, though it may have not been this particular Edmund. He became Sheriff of Essex and brought the manor of Stanesgate in Steeple Morden, on 10 March 1544.

Mary, born c.1528, married Sir Thomas Wrothe, a knight and lawyer, who was also a member of the court and one of the named members to be called to Edward VI's council if he was needed. He was also on the commission for hearing, examining, and ordering suits.[4] His marriage rights were sold by Cromwell to Rich in 1538.[5] He had probably set his sights on Wroth for one of his daughters. They had 14 children. A strong supporter of the reformed faith, Wroth, Mary and their family emigrated to Europe and only returned on the accession of Elizabeth I. Mary survived Wroth and is mentioned in his will of 1573. Rich, through his role as Chancellor of Augmentations, would acquire various manors for them to live in.

Dorothy, born c.1529, married Francis Barley of Kenton, Hereford[6] before 1567. They had at least one daughter, Lucy, who was born before 1567 (she is named in Rich's will as a beneficiary). Rich arranged and endorsed this match, for which he was granted Barley's wardship on 20 November 1536.

Anne, born c.1530, married Thomas Pygot of Stratton, Bedford[7] before 1549. Along with their daughter, Dorothy, they were named beneficiaries in Rich's will. Their marriage produced eight children. Anne died before Thomas, sometime after 1567.

Audrey/Ethelreda, born c.1530, married Robert Drewry, son and heir to Sr William Drewry of Halsted,[8] Suffolk in 1541[9]. They had 12 children between 1541 and 1557, when Robert died.[10]

Elizabeth, born c.1532, married Robert Payton of Islam, Cambridge[11] (JP and Sheriff of Cambridge), sometime before 1558. They had three sons and three daughters. Robert was a figure of high standing and in October 1559 he sat on the commission to inquire into lands taken by the Crown from the bishopric of Ely.[12]

Winifred, born c.1533, was first married to Sir Henry Dudley sometime before 1543 (he died in the Battle of Boulogne). She married the second time, around 1544, to Roger North, son and heir to St Edward North.[13] She and Roger are both mentioned in her father's will. North was a member of government and joined Queen Elizabeth's household when she was anointed.[14] They had three sons and one daughter, all born by 1556. He became a puritan.

Frances, born c.1539, married John, Lord Darcy of Cheche,[15] by 1559. They had at least two daughters, one called Elizabeth. They are both mentioned in Rich's will. She died in 1581 and is buried in St Peter and Paul Churchyard, St Osyth.

Rich's youngest daughter, Barbara, born c.1546, is thought to have joined Syon nunnery, which may be why she is not mentioned in Rich's will, or she may have passed away before Rich's death.

Rich's first-born son and heir was Hugh Rich, born c.1536. He was married to Anne Wentworth before 1554, but their marriage did not produce any children. He was made a Knight of the Bath at the coronation of Queen Mary in 1553. Hugh died in 1554.

His third son, Thomas Rich, was most likely born in the late 1530s. There is note that he married a daughter of someone named Fisher.[16] He may have had children, but the records are not clear. He is not mentioned in his father's will, which means he died before his father.

Robert Rich (son)

Robert Rich, born around 1537, became heir to Rich's titles and most of his estates after the death of Hugh in 1554. Whereas his father had worked his way up to his wealth and status, Robert was born into it, and may have even felt entitled as a result.

He married Elizabeth Baldry[17] sometime before 1554. She was the daughter of George Baldrey, Esq, of Hadleigh, Suffolk. They had three sons, Richard, Robert and Edwin, and one daughter, Elizabeth.[18] His eldest son, Richard, married Katherine Knyvet but died before his father. As with his father, Richard, his second born son, Robert, would go on to inherit the title.

Robert doesn't seem to have inherited his father's talent for the law and politics, and did not rise in the Tudor court as much as his father may have wanted him too. He was made a Knight of the Bath in 1558 and was a commissioner at the trial of the Duke of Norfolk in 1572.

What we do know of Robert was that in 1578 there was a dispute recorded between himself and Edward Windham,[19] which led to skirmishes in the street between their servants. Edward Windham was attacked In broad daylight in Fleet Street by 25 retainers of Rich, urged on by their master with bloodthirsty cries of 'drawe villains, drawe and kill him'. Windham responded by firing pistols towards Robert, who then fled into the French ambassador's house.[20] What had caused this falling out is not known, but the outcome led to Windham being imprisoned.[21] Either he was the one at fault or Robert had friends in the right places, like his father, or because of who his father's reputation. (This brawl was not an isolated incident, they frequently occurred in Fleet Street and the Strand).[22]

Robert died on 27 February 1581, and was outlived by his wife for another two decades. He is buried along with his father in Holy Cross Church, Felsted.

Robert Rich (grandson)

Robert's heir, and heir to the Rich estates, was another Robert, born sometime in December 1559. He was known as Baron Rich from 1581 until 1618, when he was granted the title of Earl of Warwick which he held until his death on 24 March the following year.

His marital life was not as smooth as his father's and grandfather's. He first married Penelope Devereux in 1581.[23] She was an attendant to Queen Elizabeth and was the daughter of Walter of Deveraux, 1st Earl of Essex. The marriage was an interesting one but certainly not a love match. It is mentioned that she was against marrying Robert and had her sights set elsewhere as she was from a family of higher standing. However, differences aside, at the start both did their duty in the marriage, with Penelope often being able to attend court, where she was very popular, and when she was not in attendance to the queen, she would split her time between St Bartholomew's and Leighs priory.

Robert would join Penelope and her brother, Essex, in writing to King James VI of Scotland, in 1589, pledging their support for him to be successor to the English Crown, an act that could be seen as treason. Robert managed to escape punishment, but Essex was sent to the Tower and put on trial, with Robert as one of the judges. Penelope was placed under house arrest and was later released. Robert divorced her in 1605 following the discovery of her adulterous affair with Charles Blount, 8th Baron Mountjoy.

Their marriage produced three sons and four daughters: Robert Rich, born c.1587, future 2nd Earl of Warwick; Henry Rich, born c.1590, granted the title the 1st Earl of Holland; Sir Charles Rich, born c.1592, died without children in 1627; Lettice Rich, born c.1594, married twice; Penelope Rich, born c.1595, married Gervase Clifton, 1st Baronet {of what?};

Essex Rich, born c.1597, married Sir Thomas Cheek; Isabella Rich, born c.1600, married Sir John Smythe.

Robert did not have a huge ego and never expected to rise to great heights in the court, because he was a second son. However, on the death of his brother, his father's titles and estates would pass to him, changing his career entirely. Up until that point he was following a career as an MP in the House of Commons. His second marriage was to Frances Wray, a widower, in 1616, but it was a short-lived union as Rich died the same year. Frances did not remarry and lived the rest of her life as a wealthy widow, passing away in 1634.

In religion Rich, like others around him, was turning towards Puritanism, which led him into disputes with John Aylmer, Bishop of London. A number of Richard Rich's descendants became Puritans. It would be this Robert Rich who was responsible for the building of the Rich tomb at Felsted Church.

Robert Rich, 2nd Earl of Warwick (great grandson)

Great grandson to Rich and eldest son of Richard Rich and Penelope Deveraux, Robert, 2nd Earl of Warwick, as he later became, was born in either May or June 1587.[24] One interesting thing to note about Robert was that he was a Puritan. An experienced naval officer, he was a founding member of the Bermuda Company for the plantation of the Somers Islands.[25] He would find himself traveling to the New World under the Virginia Company and being involved in the establishment of the Providence Island colony in the West Indies.

He married three times, first to Frances Hatton in 1605, which produced three daughters and two sons, including the heir, another Robert, born 1611, who would continue the Rich name and legacy. Their other children included Anne, born 1604, Lucy in 1615, Frances in 1621, and Charles around 1623. His second marriage was to Susan Halliday and his third marriage was to Eleanor Radcliffe.

As expected of a man of his standing, he stood as a member of parliament for Mallon from 1604 until 1611, and in 1614 for Essex. He was a great lover of the arts, drama, and the tiltyard. Unlike his great grandfather, Warwick was not going to try and serve his king no matter what. Because of his Puritan beliefs, Warwick found himself on the opposing side to King Charles I in 1640 at the outbreak of the English Civil War. His grandson and heir, (another) Robert, would be married to Oliver Cromwell's daughter, Francis, although the marriage was short-lived. He was appointed commander of the English naval fleet in 1642.

He died on 19 April 1658 and is buried in Felsted Church. Oliver Cromwell is said to have been saddened by his death.

Henry Rich, 1st Earl of Holland

Warwick's brother, Henry, 1st Earl of Holland, was born sometime around August 1590. Raised to be a member of the gentry, and prepared for life as a courtier, Henry is described as 'extravagant, decorative, quarrelsome and highly successful.'[26] He attended Emmanuel College, Cambridge, and lived in France before following a military career in the Netherlands.[27] Henry befriended King Charles I and became one of his favourites in court. He was entrusted with being involved in the negotiations around Charles' marriage to Henrietta Maria of France in 1625. As a result of this friendship, Henry found himself on opposite sides to his brother when the civil war broke out in 1642. He managed to escape being put on trial in September 1643, but did not learn his lesson and when the second civil war broke out in 1648 he was arrested by the parliamentarians and put on trial for treason. He was executed on 9 March 1649, in Westminster.

He married Isabel Cope, which brought with it a large estate in Kensington, which was renamed Holland House. They had a number of children, of which Charles Darwin is a descendant.

Richard Rich (illegitimate son)

Rich also had an illegitimate son, also called Richard, whom he acknowledged. On Rich's death, this son was given legacies and guardians, and had his education arranged in the common law. Rich even provided instruction for his marriage:

> [to] provide or buy one woman ward or some other woman having manees and lands of value of £200 yearly for a marriage to Richard, and shall pay his at marriage £2,500; and if he refuse to marry her or if no marriage shall be provided they shall pay him £21,000 and sell the ward or other woman if any such provided to any other person to the uttermost advantage to the performance of my will.[28]

He married Jane Machel[29] in 1574, and had one son, Nathaniel, and a daughter, Margaret (married name Wroth).

Richard adopted the Protestant faith and even held sermons in the great hall of Leighs, the home of his half-brother. He died in 1598, at Leighs, where his two children, Nathaniel and Margaret, were in attendance with their mother.

Nathaniel Rich (grandson)

Son and heir of Richard (illegitimate son) was Nathaniel Rich. Born in 1585, and though an MP, he is mainly remembered for being a merchant and adventurer. He was a member of the House of Commons on and off between 1614 and 1629,[30] representing Totnes in Devon in 1614, East Retford,[31] Nottinghamshire, in 1621, and Harwich, Essex, in 1626 and 1628,[32] among others. He was knighted at Hatton House by King James I on 8 November 1617.[33] Other roles he held were Commissioner of the Sewers, in. Essex, from 1625 until his death, and deputy governor of Providence Island, in America, from 1630 until his death.[34] He and his sister, Margaret, were present at the death of their father, so it seems the Rich family, both legitimate and illegitimate, may have been close.

Nathaniel followed in the Rich footsteps and had legal training, entering Gray's Inn on 2 February 1610.[35] Perhaps influenced by his cousin, Robert,

2nd Earl of Warwick, he bought shares in the Virginia Company and was active in expanding into America, working alongside his cousin.

He died sometime around May 1646, in Massachusetts. In his will he left some money to his Rich relations, but also left money and land in Bermuda to go towards local schools.[36] He is buried in Standon Massey, Essex, England, where he owned the manor since 1610.

Nathaniel Rich (great grandson)

Son of Richard (illegitimate) Rich's second son, another Robert, Colonel Nathaniel Rich (as he was later to become) was born in Felsted around 1620. He was another member of the Rich family to be actively involved in the English Civil War.

Educated at Felsted school, Nathaniel became a Puritan and graduated from St Catherine's College, Cambridge, before following in the Rich family footsteps once more and training as a lawyer at Gray's inn from August 1639.[37] He married Elizabeth Hampden, and she bore him three children. After her death he married a second time to Elizabeth Kerr, which produced no issue.

At the outbreak of the English Civil War, Nathaniel sided with Cromwell. He enlisted his own personal group of soldiers who fought at Powick Bridge in September, Edgehill in October 1642, and Marton Moor in July 1644. He would be given the rank of lieutenant colonel[38].

At the restoration of Charles II in 1660 he was pardoned, most likely as his name was not one of the ones of the execution warrant of Charles I. However, he was arrested in January 1661 due to a small uprising by Thomas Veneer. He was released without charge in 1665 and lived the rest of his days quietly on his estate in Standon, Essex, which he had inherited from his uncle (and possible namesake), Nathaniel Rich. He died between October 1700 and 1702.

* * *

The Rich line continued down the direct route with the title of Earl of Warwick passing from male heir to male heir as expected. In 1673 Charles Rich, 4th Earl of Warwick (great-great grandson of Rich) died without any male issue. The title passed to his cousin, Robert Rich but the estates, including that of Leighs, were left to his widow. On her death in 1678 we see the beginning of the break-up of the vast estates that Richard Rich had built in the mid-1500s. The Rochford estate was sold to Daniel Finch, 2nd Earl of Nottingham, who was a son-in-law to Mary, widow of Charles Rich, and the Leighs estate was sold to Guys Hospital in 1753. The Earl of Warwick title would cease to exist by 1759.

Although no direct male line exists today, Rich has many descendants through his daughters and grand-daughters.

Richard Rich and Essex

It has already been noted that Rich accumulated a large property portfolio, a large proportion of which was situated in Essex. His principal residence, Leighs Priory, was in Little Leighs near Chelmsford, and Rochford Hall, where he died, was southeast of Leighs, and also in Essex. Rich would not be alone in having his principal residence in Essex. His colleague and sometime friend Thomas Audley's main home was Audley End, in Saffron Walden, along with a vast number of other sites. It is likely Rich followed Audley's example in buying up land and property there,[1] and between the two of them they managed most of the county as landlords and upholders of the law and the monarch's wishes. Other leading men of the court who also resided in Essex included William Marney (Layer Marney) and William Petre (Ingatestone Hall). Due to the county's proximity to London, Essex was an ideal location for those wishing to be near their monarch.

Land ownership was just to having a home and base, it was a means of exerting one's authority and power, as well as a means of generating additional income. It was the expected thing for a member of the gentry to own land. It was seen as a show of wealth, social power and influence, a form of PR to those visiting.[2] Land ownership, in short, was the source of all social, military and political power and wealth.[3]

A man's primary residence and estate was his powerhouse, a base where one could rule like a little king. The architecture and design of the building, both inside and out, was a tool for propaganda,[4] to give the impression of one's social standing (even if it were not always correct, for example Ightham Motes' owner Richard Clement displayed symbols of the king throughout even though he was never blessed with a visit by King Henry VIII). In the same way that a noble or member of the gentry would dress to show off their wealth, the architecture of a house did the same job. It was a form of theatre, as well as advertising the common values and culture of a well-ordered society.

It would take Rich at least 25 years, and more, to build his portfolio, which included Prittlewell Priory, Hadleigh Castle, Leighs, and Rochford Hall which he bought from Henry Carey in 1552.[5] Rich spent thousands off pounds on buying properties in Essex, in addition to land in other counties. Some of the land and estates he held onto, having tenants living on them and farming the land, while others he would sell on or even exchange for other properties more suited to his needs.

The grant of Leighs Priory in 1536 was soon followed by another 15 in the same year, with 35 in 1537, 75 in 1538 and 112 in 1539. It seems that Rich wanted to establish himself and his place in Essex. He would not be alone in doing this, others such as Audley and Sir William Peter had also established or were beginning to establish a base in Essex.

Leighs Priory

Rich was granted Leighs by King Henry VIII upon his appointment as Chancellor of the Court of Augmentations in 1537. It was the first of his Essex estates. As the name indicates, Leighs was initially a priory, which had been established in 1220 for Augustinian friars. It was closed when the dissolutions began in 1536, and Rich had no doubt already set his eyes on it. Leighs had been part of the Syon estate, along with Grancourts, which was also acquired by Rich. It consisted of the priory and the land around it, including 1000 acres of pasture, 200 acres of wood and 40 acres of furze. At the time of the dissolution the estate produced an income of 114l. 4d (about £50,312 at today's value[6]).

> *25th May 1536*
> Richard Rich, Chancellor of the Court of Augmentation. Grant of the site… of the house or priory of Lighes, Essex, the church, messuages, & belonging thereto in Parva Leighes, the manors of Lighes alias Lighes Parva, Magna Lighes, Folsted, and Fyfeld, Essex;…and the manors of Lighes Camset, Bernes, and Herons…Annual value, 26l. 7s. 6d (£11,638 roughly in today's currency) ; rent, 52s. 9d.[7]

The Priory had an unusually large chapel, with the high altar being dedicated to St John the Evangelist, while additional small chapels were dedicated to

St Anne and our Lady Mary. The entrance is thought to have been where the gatehouse stands today. It was situated along the River Ter, which Rich used to create an elaborate drainage system, parts of which are still in existence today, and it ran from mill pond towards the river. There were 12 lakes, stretching over 2.5 km[8], which provided the estate with fish as well as an impressive landscape.

When Rich was granted possession of the priory he tore most of it down (it was already in some state of disrepair by this point) and rebuilt it using some of the existing materials. He wanted to make his own statement. The basic footprint was the main house surrounded by an inner and outer courtyard, with the gatehouse as the showpiece, both with octagonal turrets. The inner gatehouse was three stories, higher than the outside gatehouse. The former entrance can be retraced today by following a bridleway called the causeway. The route curves up to and beyond the park lodge to reach a large flat plateau. Here, it runs dead straight on a low embankment. At the plateau's northern edge, the towers and roofs of Leighs Priory and the chain of lakes in Pond Park in the valley of the River Ter would have come dramatically into view.[9] Approaching the inner courtyard, access is through a turreted inner red-brick gateway, with tall, mullioned windows and octagonal towers. The great hall would have replaced the priory itself, with a kitchen wing to the south. Where the chapel once stood was converted into the privy range, where Rich and his family slept and which looked onto the gardens. When having his new home built, Rich may have taken inspiration from other large grand houses such as Great Chatfield and South Wraxall.

After Rich died, Leighs stayed in the family until 1753 when it was sold to Guy's Hospital. They rented the property out as a private residence, and at some point much of the house that Rich created was demolished, with the remainder being used as a farmhouse and farming land until the end of 1905. Montagu Edward Hughes-Hughes, a retired stockbroker from London, bought the site for his family home. He died in 1938, but his third wife continued to live at Leighs. In the late 1980s it was purchased by the Country House Weddings Group and in 1995 it became the first country house in England to be granted a licence to conduct civil ceremonies, which it continues to be until this day.

There are some parts of Rich's great house which survive in what is known as the main house today. There are some surviving foundations of the priory to the east of the existing building, and some of the foundations of Rich's grand house are exposed in the gardens. It was granted Grade I-listed status by Historic England in 1967. The grounds can be visited and enjoyed, though the house itself can be visited by appointment only, and the gatehouse, sadly, is not accessible at all.

Felsted estate and lands

Rich not only acquired the priory and its grounds but also a vast amount of the surrounding area. All the land located between the A120, A130 and A131, including great Waltham, all belonged to the estate, including a number of other smaller estates which once were part of the priory, including the manors of Great and Little Leighs, the two manors in Felsted itself, and Enfield Manor, which was granted to Rich in 1541.

Felsted School was founded by Rich in 1564. The school room and lynch gate, along with the schoolmaster's house were all given Grade II*-listed status in 1952. Where the old schoolroom sits is a porch which was once part of a mediaeval shopping centre and where 20 white and 20 red herrings were distributed from a hatch during Lent at the request of Rich (it later became the herring dole of £35 a year from the governors of Felsted School).

Nearby sits the Holy Cross Church (grade I-listed), the final resting place of Richard Rich. The church dates back to the 12th century, with later alterations to the structure. It has Romanesque features and is built of rubble, flint and brick with tile and stone dressings. The south chapel, where Rich and his son Robert are entombed, is of clunch ashlar stone. Buried in the church itself are Rich's wife, Elizabeth, Thomas Rich, son of Robert Rich (died 1564), Richard Rich son of Robert (died 1580), Robert Rich (died 1581), Robert Lord Rich, Earl of Warwick (died 1619), Anne Rich, wife of Robert Lord Rich (died 1638), and other later Rich family members.

Felsted Bury, to the northwest of Leighs Priory, came into the ownership of Rich as it was part of the Syon Convents lands. The last abbess of Syon was Agnes. In 1538 she alienated the manor to Rich, along with the 'messuage in Felsted…certain lands, meadow in Felsted, Barneston, Stebbynge, Plecy,

Magna and Parva Dunmowe, Magna and Parva Waltham, Magna and Parva Lighes, Magna and Parva Reyne, Alba and Nigra Notley, Branktre, Bokynge, Maplested.'[10]

Felsted Bury was not as grand as Felsted Manor. The house formed an L shape with wings to the north and west. Rich's friend John Winsome lived there and farmed the land in 1564. There have been various alterations over the years, and it remained in the Rich family until 1678.

Little Park Farm in Great Waltham is dated back to 1295 and was part of the Leighs Priory estate, which is why it came into the hands of Rich. It was initially a deer park for hunting and linked to Pleshley Castle estate, which was held by Humphrey de Bohun, Earl of Hereford. It then came under the ownership of the Crown before being taken over by the Warner family around 1364.[11] On taking ownership of the park, Rich extended his own estate making a larger area for him to hold hunting parties and most likely to provide a new access route to Leighs. He kept the estate's traditional landscape and ancient hedgerows. It is mentioned that there may have been a wooden chapel on the estate, opposite the lodge (where the farmhouse stands[12]), which is referred to as Little Chapel.

Today, the farmhouse still stands, with parts dating back to the 14th century. The large chimney and its great fireplace were added in the 16th century. It is thought the initial building was used as overnight accommodation for hunting parties. On an upstairs fireplace is carved the coat of arms of the Devereux family, which relates to Rich's and Devereux's family joining in marriage through Rich's grandson and Walter Devereux's daughter Penelope. The estate became a working farm in the 17th century, then in 1720 it came under the ownership of Guy's Hospital Trust, who had additions made to the house. Today, it is privately owned with a Grade II-listed status. Rich also acquired large estates and hunting parks as well. Pleshley Park, once a deer park and managed by the High Constable of England, was acquired in 1547. Pond Park, located less than a mile to the northwest of Leighs Priory, and covering 471 acres, also came into Rich's possession.

Absol Park

The earliest reference to Absol Park, located near Felsted, was in 1279, when it was owned by Humphrey de Bohun, although it may have originated pre-conquest and been part of the manor of Wulfwin known as Udecas Hall. By 1438 it was absorbed into the Duchy of Lancaster through a marriage in 1380 of Mary de Bohun to Henry Bolingbroke (future King Henry IV). It was a moated house, and the estate was a deer park consisting of 271 acres. It came into Rich's hands in 1538 when Charles Brandon sold it to him, and was incorporated into his vast estate of Leighs. It remained in the Rich family until the 17th century when it seems to have been divided between the Earl of Manchester and the remainder to Guy's Hospital. Today, there is 17th-century farmhouse on the land, which is believed to have replaced an earlier building. The farmhouse was granted Grade II-listed status in December 1952 by Historic England.

Hatfield Broad Oak (Hatfield Regis/Hatfield Bury)

Hatfield Great Park and Chase dates back to pre-conquest England (in 1066 it was Harold Godwinson's largest manor). It passed into the hands of Robert de Gernom, the Steward of the Great Forest of Essex, and was then under the ownership of various members of the nobility and gentry, including Isabel Bruce (widow of Robert the Bruce), and Humphrey de Bohun, before being acquired by the Crown and then sold to Rich, along with the hunting park and forest, by King Edward IV in 1547. Its value at the time was £80 9s 8d (around £22,108.67 in today's money). Robert Rich sold it to Francis Barrington in 1612, and he owned it 1836. From the 18th century onwards the estate, around 280 acres, was referred to as Town Farm.

The building in existence today has parts dating back to the 15th century, including the hall. The chimney stack was added in the 17th century and included a two-storey kitchen range. A fire broke out in 1972 causing serious damage to the south side, which was then rebuilt to match what once stood. The two barns which still stand date back to the 15th century, one of which now consists of three flats.[13]

Moreton

Dating back as far as 1066, Moreton was held by William de Sochies[14] in 1086 and was acquired by the d'Avranches family by 1212. By the 1400s it had been separated and consisted of two separate manors: Bourchier's, or Nether Hall, and Ladyhall, or Upper Hall.

In 1342 Nether Hall came into the hands of Robert Bourchier (whose family line would eventually be created the Earls of Essex) and it was William Parr, husband of his descendant, Anne Bourchier (daughter to Henry Bourchier, 2nd Earl of Essex), who sold it to Rich in 1542, after which time it became known as Nether Hall.

Rich was endowed the Chantry of Felsted, with 55 acres of land at Moreton. The hall stayed in the Rich family until 1608 when it was conveyed to Robert Bourne. It changed hands at various times over the next few centuries and was mainly used as a home and for farming. In August 1900 the house was put up for auction along with 216 acres of land. The farm was listed as separate from the manor itself, which was brought by the Reverend F. W. Bussell. The current farmhouse dates back to the 18th century, with later 19th century additions.

The other half of Moreton passed into the hands of William de Clynton, Earl of Huntingdon, and then John, Lord Mowbray. By 1383 it was known as Ladyhall and was owned by the Dukes of Norfolk. It was Thomas, 8th Duke of Norfolk, who granted Ladyhall, now known as Upper Hall, to Richard Rich. Like Nether Hall, Upper Hall followed a similar pattern, with different owners. Around1846, Upper Hall was dissolved, leaving Nether Hall as the only manor in Moreton.

Rochford Hall

The place of Rich's death, Rochford Hall is listed in the Domesday book of 1066, when it was under the ownership of a high-ranking noble, Sweyne, whose son changed the family name to 'de Essex. It entered Crown hands and was then passed back and forth between various lords until, in 1420, it was inherited by James Butler, 4th Earl of Ormond. While under the ownership of Butler the manor was rebuilt from red brick and ragstone, and evidence of this survives today in the octagonal chimneys and turrets. Rochford Hall was then acquired by the Boleyn family in 1515. Thomas Boleyn, father to Anne, made Rochford his home on 26 October 1517, and on his death, it passed to Mary Carey, his only surviving child. Mary died at the hall on 19 July 1543, and all her properties went to her 18-year-old son, Henry, from her first marriage. The hall was set in an eight-acre walled park and was moated on three sides. The northern part of the wall still survives today.

Henry Carey made some changes to the mansion. Fragments of carved stonework within the walls show that the materials used during these alterations would have come from some of those monasteries which were dissolved during the Tudor period. William Stafford, Henry's stepfather, sold some of the local church bells to pay for repairs to sea walls. Henry sold Rochford Hall and its estate to Rich, and it stayed in the Rich family until 1712 when it was sold for a second time.

The new owners were the Child family (who had already bought some other properties that once belonged to the Rich family). It was under their ownership that, in 1760, a fire broke out, destroying at least half of the great mansion. The damage was so severe that the south side of the building was torn down, and parts of the north end were turned into barns while some parts were left derelict.

Over the following years the manor passed to various owners, mainly through inheritance, and parts of it became derelict and in disrepair. In 1867 it was put up for sale for a third time. It was now known as Rochford Hall Farm and was brought by James Tabor, a farmer with Essex roots. His nephew wrote:

> it was scarcely fit for anyone to live in, and it would have cost a very large sum to restore it properly, but the owners objected to its being left derelict… so Uncle James made one or two rooms habitable. He could well afford or restore Rochford Hall to something like its previous grandeur, or to build a 'mansion for himself…be he kept to one room.[15]

During its time as a farm many of the farmhands who worked there slept in the east wing. In 1896 the east wing and a large part of the parkland was let to Rochford Golf Club. From the early 1900s the Talbots ceased to work the farm, and a number of tenants took up the work instead. Sometimes there would be tours of the upper floors of the hall for a small fee to the public. Graffiti from these tours can still be seen today.

During the Second World War some German prisoners of war who were housed in what is now Rochford Hospital worked on the farm and repaired the hedges. During the 1980s master craftsman Malcolm Ginns took on the job of restoring some of the barns at the hall. He built four private properties with gardens. Today, Rochford Hall is a Grade I-listed four-bedroom house with a barn annex and swimming The oldest part of the building still in existence dates from 1216. The hall would have been built of red brick and Kentish ragstone. It had three or four courtyards and three, possibly more, octagonal towers, perpendicular door arches, and typical Tudor twisting chimneys. There would also have been a great hall and a chapel. The hall is a Grade I-listed building, granted on 4th December 1951, number 1112586 and scheduled ancient monument. It is privately owned with parts being accessible to members of Rochford Golf club who own the land.

Wanstead

There is thought to have been some form of occupation on this site dating as far back as Roman times. The area is listed in the Domesday book as 'Wanstead, under the ownership of the bishop of London, and managed by Ralph son of Brien. There were 3 villages and 8 small holders with ploughland, woodland, a mill and salthouse and it had an annual value of 2 pounds.' The precise location of the mediaeval manor is not known for certain. In 1509 the area was brought by King Henry VIII, who had the land enclosed, and had the manor developed into a royal hunting lodge, which, by 1549, was in ruins. This was when Rich bought it and built Wanstead House, redeveloping the land into one of the largest in Essex. From 1567 he leased it to James, Lord of Danbury. He then sold it to Robert Dudley in 1578, with subsequent owners being Charles Blount, George Villiers and Sir Henry Mildmay.[16]

What exists today is the result of the Child family who were the initial tenants in 1667, and actual owners in 1673. Various members of the family developed and changed the landscape, and the house was completely rebuilt by Sir Richard Child, after which it was considered one of the greatest mansions of its time. Sadly, it was demolished in 1823.[17]

Rich's other properties (but not all) include:

Beamish Hall, under Faversham Abbey, granted in 1539 and sold the same year.

Belstead Hall, under Holy Trinity London, bought in 1546 and sold the same year.

Bois Hall, originally under the ownership of Westminster Abbey, was granted to Rich in 1542.

Brayhams Manor, in 1540.

Cowbridge Manor, under Stratford Abbey, granted in 1545 and sold the same year.

Earls Hall, bought in 1559.

Eastwood Manor, granted in 1551.

Franches Manor, bought in 1546.

Glanville and Laver, bought in 1540.

Hapleston, bought in 1540.

Hockley Hall, under Baring Abbey and brought in 1558.

Hutton Manor, under the ownership of Battle Abbey and brought in 1539.

Imbers Manor, under the ownership of Westminster Abbey, was built in 1542 and sold in the same year.

Milton Hall/Middleton, under Church ownership and was granted to Rich on 20 January 1545. A house now stands on its site.

Mulsham Hall, bought in 1540 and sold the same year.

Mynchens Manor, under Clerkenwell Monastery, granted in 1539 and sold the same year.

Passfield Manor, bought in 1540.

Patching Hall, bought in 1548

Prittlewell Priory

Shelly Hall, bought in 1538.

Shoebury Hall, under the ownership of Prittlewell Priory, granted in 1537.

Southchurch Hall, under Canterbury Christ Church, granted in 1545, along with **Lolling Hall and Stistead Hall.**

Stansgate Manor, under Canterbury Christ Church and bought in 1545.

Tillingham Hall, under Coggeshall Abbey, bought in 1554

Waltham Bury Manor, bought in 1539.

Whitley Manor, granted in 1540.

Wood Hall, bought in 1548.

Richard Rich in Screen and Print

As we have seen Rich, was a key player in many events of the Tudor era. Because of that, he has appeared in print and on screen in dramatisations of the period, and though never the main character, he is often one who impacts the plot and those who come into contact with him, and often portrayed as a scheming villain. No study of the man is complete without looking at his legacy on screen and page.

'A Man for All Seasons'

Initially a play, 'A Man for all Seasons', by Robert Bolt, was first published in 1960 and debuted on stage at the Globe theatre on 1 July 1960, directed by Noel Willman. It is the classic dramatisation of Sir Thomas More's historic conflict with Henry VIII; a compelling portrait of a courageous man who died for his convictions.

Bolt depicts Rich as perjuring himself against More in order to become Attorney-General for Wales. The first time Rich is introduced in the play is as a man who really wants to be part of the goings-on at court and uses More to get his foot in the door. Later he is approached by Cromwell who wants to know more about Thomas More. Rich obliges and is rewarded. Rich was first played on stage by John Brown.

In 1966 the play was adapted for the big screen. More was played by Paul Schofield (who played More in the original stage play), Cromwell by Leo McKern, and Rich was played by John Hurt. The film won six Oscars, including Best Picture, and in 1999 the BFI named it the 43rd greatest British film of all time. Rich is not played as a stereotypical villain, but one out for himself. In the scene where More confronts him, Rich cannot look him in the eye, knowing what he has done.

Both play and screen adaptations are worth watching, but Bolt shows a very one-sided view of More. Those who were responsible for his death, such as Rich, are therefore seen as opponents to More. Rich is depicted as not being the leader of More's downfall but a man willing to do what it took to gain power for himself. It was Cromwell who was the architect of More's downfall, using Rich as a means to this. Rich appears as someone not necessarily able to build a career on his own merits, and looks to those in higher positions, like More, to begin with, and Cromwell, to enrich him. One of More's biographers, Richard Marius, has even said that 'Bolt's idolatry of More's character' was inexcusable.

'Richard Rich – The Man Who Kept His Head'

> *Baron Rich is now 71 years old and nearing death at his Rochford manor. His eldest daughter, the faithful Joan, has spent her life caring for the extensive Rich estates and her 16 siblings. She convinces Rich to speak to her of his life's memories. She knows many notable figures from his years in power are writing memoirs and histories of the time and wants to record her father's own words.*

Thoroughly researched, this is an interesting take on Rich and his life by its author Elizabeth Engebretson. She tries to give an explanation for Rich's actions, how he hated More for looking down on him, and how Rich hated himself for his part in Cromwell's downfall. Though part-fiction, the book's inclusion of his later life, and his relationships with his family, helps to establish a more human Rich and a relatable man, rather than the villain of the piece.

'Shardlake' series by C. J. Sansom (2004–2018)

In 2006, the late author C. J. Sansom published *Sovereign*, the third book in his Shardlake series, in which Rich first appears. All the books tend to involve a crime or mystery, which its protagonist, hunchback lawyer Mathew Shardlake, attempts to solve. Rich is one of the villains of the novels, but it is in *Sovereign* where his character has more of the limelight. He is portrayed as we have come to expect, a cruel, greedy man who only looks out for himself with little regard for the law which he is meant to uphold.

As the novels progress and time passes, Rich becomes more powerful, and consequently, more sinister and corrupt, becoming the arch-nemesis of Shardlake. The sixth novel, *Lamentation*, opens with the execution of Anne Askew and continues with Kathryn Parr calling for help from Shardlake to help her prevent the Catholic faction from plotting her downfall. Rich, of course, plays a big part in this novel.

The Shardlake series gives us another interpretation of Rich. Sansom certainly portrays Rich's villainous streak, and his greed and his lack of morals and conscience. He even says to Shardlake at one point, 'Those with conscience are too obsessed with the rightness of their cause to survive, in the end,'[1].' which I which sums him up very well.

'The Tudors' (2008 and 2009)

Released in 2007 The Tudors, produced by Showtime, ran for four seasons and covered the reign of King Henry VIII, who is played by Jonathan Rhys-Myers. It is not historically accurate but certainly brought the characters from this era to life.

Richard Rich, played by Rod Hallett, appears in seasons 2–4 of the series, with more appearances in the later seasons. Initially, he is loyal to Cromwell and seems to agree with his religious views and how the monasteries were corrupt and against the idolatry of Catholicism. He is involved in the questioning of Anne Boleyn's ladies, seemingly sympathetic and gentle towards them. His conversation with More is interesting as it is played as just one lawyer to another with no sinister intent. On leaving, he states to More that his work is done, giving the impression of a man who regretted that More engaged in the conversation and said what he did as it meant that Rich would have to report back to the king, even though he did not want to. The show seems to push the idea that it was the determination of King Henry VIII for More be executed rather than have Cromwell or Rich be the mastermind behind it. When Cromwell is charged, Rich is confronted by Seymour about their friendship. Rich's response is similar to what Cranmer had written to King Henry VIII in 1540. It could be possible the writers used Cranmer's words and gave them to Rich, like what sometimes happens in dramas based on real life. After Cromwell's fall he seems to change allegiance and in the last season is allied with the Catholics. He questions some of Catherine Howard's ladies, gently once more. However, he does not shy away from torturing Askew. In one scene he informs Princess Mary of the death of Chapuys and tells her things are in motion to stop the 'heretics' rise to dominance. She asks if he is Catholic, to which he nods 'yes'.

In 'The Tudors' Rich's character is a mixed bag. Although he is not the dastardly villain often depicted, he is still shown as one who was comfortable to change allegiances to suit his own ends. His involvement in More's downfall shows him in a more sympathetic light than most accounts.

Wolf Hall

Hilary Mantel's first part of her trilogy was published in 2009 (the second part is *Bring up the Bodies* (2012) and the third is *The Mirror and the Light* (2020). The books, and subsequent TV dramatisations, follow the life of Thomas Cromwell. Rich is described as 'a seasoned lawyer, Rich served as Cromwell's chief lieutenant in the dissolution of the monasteries. The pair make an effective team, but Rich's loyalty has a Machiavellian streak[2]'.

In *The Mirror and the Light (2024)* Rich, played by Tom Mothersdale, is shown as an ally of Cromwell's. More about his character and Cromwell's view of him comes to light in the final episode, when Cromwell is imprisoned in the Tower and visited by Gardiner, Norfolk, Wriothesley and Rich. Rich tries to lead the questioning, seemingly in an attempt to outsmart Cromwell, which he fails to do, and Cromwell makes him look a fool at times. Cromwell does not seem surprised at Rich's betrayal, but is more surprised at Wriothesley, who tries to tell Cromwell he is doing what he can to survive.

* * *'

'A Man for all Seasons', is, for many, their first introduction to Rich, and it will be difficult to then try and change one's opinion of him. It is a biased portrayal of him, as it is *Wolf Hall*, in which Hilary Mantell views Cromwell as the hero, doing his best for the king, with Rich being involved in Cromwell's downfall. Rich is also portrayed in a poor light in the Shardlake books, appearing as the villain to Shardlake's hero. The Tudors seems to be the only adaptation which is not biased against him, but here Rich is merely used as a tool to drive the narrative, with no explanation for the change in his religious beliefs. He may have supported the Reformation but would not had voiced the hatred towards the idolatrous ceremonies (I think anyway). I feel in one series he is written as being a supporter of the Reformation and stepping away from the Pope and in the next a staunch catholic and anti-Reformation.

Creative licence is something we must all be aware of when watching anything with some historical truth or basis to it. Richard Rich's introduction to most people will be through one of the interpretations listed above and none of them show his true self. What they all have in common, however, are the facts of his political career: his involvement in More's trial; in Cromwell's arrest; Askew's torture; and his growing wealth as a result of his actions. This is a fact that no one can defend.

The Greatest Tudor Villain?

'A time server studying to obtain the good will of all parties.' *L. Baldwin-Smith*

'Risen by means of ability and absence of scruples.' *J. Bettlet and N. Pevesner*

'He was an absolute snake.' *K. Claiden-Yardley*

'odious and unprincipled'. *A. G. Dickens*

'least endearing of Tudor personalities'. *P. Gwyn*

'Ever swinging with the political wind'. *P. Hutchinson*

'dastardly, lawyer by training, obnoxious, amoral, ruthless, climbed high on bodies of those more principled than himself'. *S. Lipscomb*

'How a man so deeply mired in corruption, treachery and perjury managed to flourish through so many different regimes is unclear. It makes it difficult to question his skills as a lawyer as his services must have made up for his shortcomings.' *R. Matthews*

'principles had no meaning for Rich'. *J. E. Oxley*

'unencumbered by any discernible principles and never too far away from charges of corruption'. *R. Young*

Above are just some examples of historians' views of Richard Rich. There is no one who can defend Rich's actions in his life; no one who can say he had good intentions and was a good man. But does that automatically make him a bad man, a man who some refer to as the greatest Tudor villain?

Rich rose in the Tudor court due to his own efforts and his knowledge of the law. He made himself of use to those in higher positions, which is how he was able to progress. Like many others, he started his career in the Inns of Court, knowing that he needed powerful patrons if he was to make something of himself. This was not new; one only needs to look at Cromwell to see how knowledge and cunning could get one a place in the court.

Rich enriched himself during the dissolution, but this was not of his own doing. It would have happened with his involvement or not. He earned his place as Chancellor of Augmentations because of his own expertise in the relevant parts of the law. He was not duly worried if the monks and nuns were corrupt; he was simply there to do his job. Rich did not enrich himself illegally, and though there were rumours of him being corrupt, no charges were ever brought. Either he was innocent or just very clever. From the dissolution he built a powerful base for himself and his growing family. He would not be alone in this; other members of the Tudor court did the same.

During the dissolution we can see signs of Rich's dislike of being told how to do his job. He knew what was best. He did not appreciate Cromwell, at times, micromanaging him. He had a job to do and wanted to do it to the best of his ability. However, he did not offend or alienate Cromwell and the two continued to work together.

What becomes apparent at this time is Rich's purpose, not just to enrich himself but to serve the Crown, more specifically his monarch, whoever it may have been. As the Tudor monarchs changed, and the course of religion swayed back and forth, so did Rich, on the outside any least, for that is what was expected of a loyal servant and also how one survived in the court. Like his peers, Rich was 'not acting solely from ambition. They had persuade themselves that it was their duty to obey the sovereign….because… [the monarch] …alone had the right to decide what religion his subjects should adopt…no loyal subject would be sent to hell if he had supported heresy only out of obedience to his prince.'[1]

Rich was a survivor through and through. There were not many who could say they survived under four Tudor monarchs, as he had. Those who still had their heads were impacted at one point or another with executions of family members, imprisonment, or even banishment from court. None of that applied to Rich. The only problem he had was with Somerset, and even then he was able to quickly get himself back on the right side. It was during Edward's reign that Rich's career reached its zenith, which is perhaps why he lost his way, and his intuitiveness on how to play the Tudor court.

Rich's involvement in More's execution, Cromwell's downfall and the torture of Askew were the defining moments in his life and all were carried out with different motives. For More and Cromwell especially, their fates were sealed by the will of the king. With or without Rich they were dead men walking once Henry had made up his mind. All that Rich did was place himself into the citation and provide the king with what he wanted, making himself useful to the one man that mattered. Cromwell knew the importance of keeping the king's ear to survive. His downfall came about because he had failed the king, and he had too many enemies at court. Rich learned from those around him. He knew how best to be in the court without being directly be in the king's line of sight, but remaining useful.

Henry VIII was a difficult master to serve, hence why so many of those close to him found themselves exiled, or worse. He was a man who expected his own way, lawful or not. He was spoiled and had a temper. He was like a toddler; if he did not get what he wanted he threw a tantrum. In addition, if he considered you a friend and you made him look foolish or feel betrayed then retribution would be swift. Everyone at court, and in the privy chamber would certainly have been aware of this, and when the wind started to change, they would turn their backs on those facing the chop, even if they were their own friends. Even Cromwell behaved in this way with the likes of More and Anne Boleyn. He did not dislike them, he was merely doing his job.

This description of Rich, written by W. C. Richardson, is particularly accurate:

> In training and fitness, the hierarchy of the Court represented a fair selection of ministerial ability. Richard Rich, the man chosen for the chancellorship, was in many respects a typical Tudor careerist, whose success already bore witness to his unusual resilience and tact. A shrewd opportunist whose ambition readily permitted him to support any policy however distasteful, he was able to co-operate remarkably well with superiors and subordinates alike. Though envied by the less fortunate and criticized by those who condemned the institution he served, contemporary accounts of him were generally not unfavourable. Historians have maligned him most, with the result that his name is still commonly associated with greed and corruption.

Rich was, in the end, a loyal servant to his monarch, whoever that may have been. He knew the key to survival was doing what they wanted, even if it meant betraying his own beliefs.

> The ancient families are always watching for a chance to promote their champion to the throne. The Seymours, the Dudleys, the Howards; in your own life you've seen their attempts at unseating the Welsh upstarts as they view the Tudors […] As soon as the occupant of the throne faltered: King Henry's health faded, King Edward's frailty increased, Queen Mary's mind slipped, one of them was always ready to pounce. The likes of Wolsey and Cromwell, Wriothesley, Audley, Cranmer, me, yes, even More were only tools to them, expendable, of no long-term importance. Oh, we were all allowed a certain amount of power and position, personal embellishments, wealth, good marriages for our children, but I, perhaps alone, knew that it all could be taken away even faster than it had been granted. I always knew where the real power lay and made certain each knew I knew and respected it.'
>
> Richard Rich in *Richard Rich – The Man who Kept his Head*

On a few occasions Rich did step out from this safety net and spoke up, but he knew it was not enough to warrant putting his life in danger. Moreover, these few occasions came later in his life and under female monarchs so perhaps he also knew he was safe from execution. I personally feel he would not have spoken out against the possible loss of his property back to the Catholic church if King Henry VIII had demanded it.

In short, Rich does deserve the label of one of the greatest Tudor villains, but he was also one of the great Tudor survivors.

Who's Who

The following is brief outline of all those mentioned in this book, including some of the titles and offices held. Its use is simply to assist with the huge number of court nobility involved in the life of Rich. Any errors made are the author's own. Those already covered in detail in the main section have been excluded from this list, along with the Tudor monarchs and Henry VIII's wives.

BARTON, Elizabeth (the nun of Kent/Holy Maid of Kent)
(1506–1534)

A domestic servant living in Kent, Barton fell ill in 1525, and it was from there she started having trances which led to her making prophecies. She came to the attention of More and the Archbishop of Canterbury in 1526, and even Henry VIII became aware of her prophesying. However, things changed in 1532 when she predicted that if Henry married Anne Boleyn he would die 'a villain's death'. She was arrested and though her jailers tried to get her to admit she was a fraud, she refused. More and Fisher were even questioned about their association with her. Barton was hanged on 20 April 1534.

BONNER, Edmund (Bishop of London)
(c.1500–1569: 1529–1530)

Chaplain to Wolsey 1529–1530; Prebend of St Paul's 1537–1539; Ambassador in Paris 1538.
Bonner attended what is now Pembroke College in 1512 where he earned a Bachelor in both Civil and Canon Law in 1519, and in 1525 was a Doctor of Civil Law. A loyal servant under King Henry VIII, Bonner was known to speak his mind and did not worry about offending others, including Stephen

Gardiner. After Henry's death and during Somerset's Protectorship, Bonner would become outspoken in accepting the Royal Supremacy and Somerset's power. He was placed in Fleet prison for two months in 1547. His refusal to accept the Act of Supremacy led to him being deprived of his bishopric in 1549, followed by a stay in Marshalsea prison. He was released when Mary became queen and restored to the bishopric of London, becoming an avid persecutor of heretics under Queen Mary, which earned him the nickname 'Bloody Bonner'. On the accession of Elizabeth, he was requested to relinquish his bishopric. He refused and as was sent to Marshalsea prison in 1560 where he remained for the rest of his life. He died on 5 September 1569 and is buried in St George's, Southwark.

BOLEYN, Jane (née Parker)
(c.1505–1542)

Wife of George Boleyn (brother of Anne). After George's execution she was absent from court for a few months trying to negotiate with her former father-in-law and Cromwell about money owed to her as a widow. She returned to court and served Jane Seymour, Anne of Cleves, and finally Catherine Howard. When Catherine was questioned and her supposed adultery was investigated, Jane was placed with her at Syon, where she was also questioned, before both of them were imprisoned in the Tower. While there she was questioned further and the stress if it all caused her to have a nervous breakdown. In 1542 she was pronounced insane. Henry had the best doctors sent to get her back to health, mainly so she could face trial for her crimes in aiding and abetting Catherine in her adulterous activities. She was eventually sentenced to beheading when Henry had the law changed so that insane people could be executed if guilty of high treason. She was beheaded on Tower green with Catherine Howard on 13 February 1542, and her body was buried in the chapel of St Peter ad Vincula.

CAREY, Henry (Lord Hunsdon)
(c.1524–1596)

Esquire of the Body 1520–28; MP for Buckingham 1547 and 1554; Carver of the Privy Chamber 1553–1558; Gentleman of the Household 1554–5; Baron Hunsdon 1559; Master of the Queen's Hawks 1560; Captain of the Gentlemen Pensioners 1564; Warden of the East Marches 1571; Lord Chamberlain of the Household 1585.

The only son of William Carey and Mary Boleyn. Although a member of the Privy Court, it was his cousin Elizabeth's ascension to the throne that really pushed Carey's career in the court. He was knighted and raised to the peerage as 1st Baron Hunsdon on 13 January 1559, in addition to receiving grants of land in numerous countries including Essex, and the manor of Hunsdon in Hertfordshire.

Carey was appointed Governor of Berwick on 25 August 1568, making him one of the most senior officials in the area. This set him on a path of regularly finding himself up north and dealing with numerous issues with the Scots, including when Mary Queen of Scots had fled Scotland. Carey was not impressed with how lenient Elizabeth was towards her and even wrote her a letter detailing this.

From 1577, when he was appointed a member of the Privy Council, Carey made it the focus of the rest of his career in the court, regularly appearing at meetings, and being involved in some of the proposed marriages of Queen Elizabeth.

Carey married Anne Morgan in 1545, who bore him 10 sons. He died on 23 June 1528 and is buried in Westminster Abbey.

CECIL, William (Baron Burghley)
(c.1520–1598)

1st Baron Burghley 1571–1598; Lord High Treasurer 1572–1598; LordPrivy Seal 1571–72 and 1590–1598; Secretary of State 1550–1553 and 1558–1572; Lord Lieutenant of Lincolnshire 1587–1598; Lord Lieutenant of Essex 1588–1598; Lord Lieutenant of Hertfordshire 1588–1598; Chancellor of the University of Dublin 1592–1598; Master of Requests 1548; MP for Stamford 1547; MP for Lincolnshire 1553, 1555 and 1559; MP for Northampton 1563.

Elizabeth I's most trusted advisor, whom she nicknamed her eyes. He served in the households of all the Tudor monarchs bar Henry VII. He went to St John's College, Cambridge. William married twice, first to Mary Cheke, with whom he had one son, and after her death he married Mildred Cooke in 1546 who bore four children. Along with Jane Grey, Cecil's wife, Mildred was considered one of the most learned ladies in England. He was imprisoned in the Tower with John Dudley but was released without charge. He is buried in St Martins, Stamford.

CHAPUAYS, Eustace
(c.1494-c.1550)

Imperial Ambassador to England in the reign of Henry VIII 1529–1536 and 1542–1545.
Kept detailed correspondence on the goings-on in the English court. Was a loyal supporter of both Catherine of Aragon and Mary Tudor.

CRANMER, Thomas (Archbishop of Canterbury)
(1489–1556)

Archbishop of Canterbury 1533–1555; Ambassador at the court of the Holy Roman Emperor 1532–1533.
A key player in the English Reformation and helped build the case against Catherine of Aragon. He was a supporter of royal supremacy. Held the role of Archbishop of Canterbury from December 1533 to December 1535 and established the first doctrinal and liturgical structures of the reformed Church of England. He published the first officially authorised vernacular service, the Exhortation and Litany. He wrote a letter to Henry VIII after finding out about Catherine Howard's extramarital affairs, which led to her arrest and execution. Under Edward Tudor he was more open in his reform and compiled the first two editions of the Book of Common Prayer. Under Mary Tudor was put on trial for heresy and treason and eventually burned at the stake. He married a woman called Joan who died in childbirth. A few years later he married Margaret, with whom he had several children, but he had to keep them hidden after the passing of the Act of Six Articles, making it illegal for a man of the cloth to marry. He appears in *Foxe's Book of Martyrs*.

DUDLEY Edmund
(c.1462–1510)

Father of John Dudley.
A trained lawyer and MP, who, along with Richard Empson, was responsible for collecting money owed to King Henry VII, including fines imposed on the men in the court for misdeeds. This role made them both very unpopular. Thus, when Henry VII died, they became the scapegoats for the strict regime the former king had imposed. The new king, Henry VIII, wanted to appease those around him and make himself popular, so he had trumped up charges brought against Empson and Dudley and they were found guilty of treason and executed on 17 August 1510.

DUDLEY, John (Earl of Warwick)
(1504–1553)

1st Duke of Northumberland 1551–1553; Earl of Warwick 1547–1553; Vice-Admiral 1537–1543; Lord Admiral 1543–1547 and 1529–1550; Governor of Boulogne 1544–1545; Lord Great Chamberlain 1547–1550; Grand Master of the Royal Household 1550–1553; Warden General of the Scottish marshes 1542–1543 and 1551–1553; Earl Marshal of England 1551; MP for Kent 1529; MP for Staffordshire 1542; Justice of the Peace for Surrey and Sussex 1531–1545, JP for Warwickshire 1532–1553; JP for Kent 1537–1553; JP for Staffordshire 1538–1553; JP for Worcestershire 1540–1553; Ambassador to Spain 1537.
Admiral, politician and member of the Tudor nobility. After the execution of his father, he became a ward of Edward Guildford and ended up training to be a soldier in France. Considered to be very skilful, especially in wrestling, archery and jousting tournaments. He married Jane Guildford (daughter of Edward) in 1525 and had 13 children, including Robert Dudley, favoured by the future Elizabeth Tudor. He led the Reformist party at the end of Henry VIII's reign. He became the unofficial ruler of England after the arrest of protector Somerset, and attempted to place Jane Grey on the throne instead of Mary, who was the rightful heir under the will of Henry VIII. This led to his arrest and execution on Tower Hill. He is buried in the Chapel of St Peter ad Vincula.

Empson, Richard
(c.1450–1510)

See DUDLEY, Edmund

FISHER, John (Bishop of Rochester)
(c.1469–1535)

Fisher was ordained as a priest in the early 1480s in York and the following decade he came to the attention of Margaret Beaufort (mother to the current king Henry VII, and grandmother to Henry VIII) who recruited him into her service where he eventually became her spiritual director. In 1504 he was recommended to King Henry VII and was created Bishop of Rochester along with being made chancellor of Cambridge University.

Although close to London, Fisher rarely took on any diplomatic and government responsibilities, choosing to focus on his role as bishop, preaching God's word and founding St John's College, Cambridge. He was opposed to the new Reformist religion and preached at the burnings of Martin Luther's books in 1521, along with being involved in some proceedings against Reformers in the 1520s.

He refused to acknowledge Henry's divorce from Catherine of Aragon. He was a huge supporter of hers and even authored a statement highlighting the validity of the marriage. This caused Henry great frustration and anger for the next six years. What caused his downfall were his visits to Elizabeth Barton, Holy Maid of Kent, who was having visions of the king's demise. As he did not declare these so-called visions, he was placed under arrest along with Barton and others under the charge of treason. His wealth and goods were confiscated, and Fisher was placed in the Tower, where attempts were made to get him to accept the king as supreme head of the Church. By not acknowledging this, he was found guilty of high treason and Henry pushed for his execution. Fisher was duly beheaded on 22 June 1535.

FOXE, John
(1516–1587)

Staunch Protestant who authored *Acts and Monuments of these Latter and Perilous Days*, known today as *Foxe's Book of Martyrs*, which details those

Protestants who suffered for their religious beliefs. It covered the period from the 14th century to the reign of Mary Tudor (1556), and was printed on the accession of Elizabeth Tudor in 1559. He was an ordained member of the Church of England for a time and became an Anglican priest in 1560, but resigned due to his puritan beliefs. Foxe fled the country when Mary came to the throne in order to escape persecution. He is buried in St Giles, Cripplegate, London.

GARDINER, Stephen
(1483–1555)

Bishop of Winchester 1531–1551 and 1553–1555; Ambassador to France 1535–1538; Secretary of State 1528–1534; Archdeacon of Taunton, Worcester and Norfolk 1526–1531; Archdeacon of Leicester; 1531; Chancellor of the University of Cambridge; Lord Chancellor 1553–1555.
In his early adult life, he was secretary to Cardinal Wolsey. Initially supportive of Henry VIII's Royal Supremacy, Gardener was a Catholic and attempted to bring England back towards Catholicism. He was involved in the writing of the Six Articles. Initially supportive of the marriage of Henry VIII to Kathryn Parr, Gardiner would eventually turn against the queen, and, along with Thomas Wriothesley, attempted to plot her downfall. As a result of his beliefs, he was imprisoned during the reign of Edward Tudor, though later rose to prominence under Mary Tudor. He was one of the leaders of the Catholic faction in court under Henry VIII and was involved in the plot to have Kathryn Parr arrested. He is buried in Winchester Cathedral.

GREY, Jane
(1537–1554)

Proclaimed Queen of England 10 July 1553–19 July 1553.
A staunch Protestant, she was sent to live in Kathryn Parr's household after being placed under the care of Thomas Seymour. She became a close friend of the dowager queen and was chief mourner at her funeral. She was used by her father and father-in-law as a pawn and was placed on the throne. She survived the initial uprising, but Mary had no choice but to execute her when another uprising was held in her name. She is buried in the chapel of St Peter ad Vincula.

HOLBEIN, Hans
(c.1497–1543)

Originally from Germany, Holbein is considered one of the greatest portrait artists of his day. He arrived in England in 1526 after being encouraged by Dutch humanist Erasmus. By 1535 he was the king's painter, receiving the patronage of Thomas Cromwell and Anne Boleyn. Some of his most famous portraits include the Whitehall mural (of which a copy survives) and the family of Henry VIII, which included Jane Seymour even though Henry was married to Kathryn Parr at the time. He painted many members of the Tudor elite during his time in England. In addition to portraits, Holbein designed decorative works such as murals, jewellery and even a fireplace.

HOWARD, Thomas (Duke of Norfolk)
(1473–1544)

Duke of Norfolk 1524–1547 and 1553–1554; Earl of Surrey 1514–1554; Lord High Admiral 1513–1525; Lord Deputy of Ireland 1522; Lord Treasurer 1533–1546; Lord High Steward 1521, 1534 and 1536; Order of St Michael 1532; Earl Marshal of England 1533–1547 and 1553–1554; Lieutenant General of the Kings Army in France 1543.

A politician, nobleman and soldier who was the head of a large family and the uncle to two of the king's wives, Anne Boleyn and Catherine Howard. He became a close friend to the king and played prominent roles in several events in his reign such as presiding over the trial of his niece Anne in 1536, shutting down the Pilgrimage of Grace, and the fall of Thomas Cromwell. He and his son fell from grace and were imprisoned in the Tower for treason in 1546, with Thomas only surviving the axe as a result of the king's death. He was a staunch Catholic and only released from prison on the ascension of Mary Tudor, rising to a prominent position once more. He married Anne of York, an aunt of the king, in 1475, and they had four children who all died in infancy. Howard then married Lady Elizabeth Stafford in 1513 and had five children with her. They formally separated sometime in the 1530s after he had installed his mistress in their household. He is buried at St Michael's Church, Framlingham, Suffolk.

Plantagenet, Arthur (Viscount Lisle)
(c.1461–1542)

Esquire of the King's Bodyguard 1509; High Sheriff of Hampshire 1514; Vice Admiral of England 1525; Lord Deputy of Calais 1533–40; Privy Councillor 1533; Lord Warden of the Cinque Ports 1536.
An illegitimate son of King Edward IV, Arthur was Henry VIIIs uncle and the two were very close. He served in the court, mainly in Calais, to the best of his ability. In 1523 he was created Viscount Lisle and was author of the Lisle letters. In 1540 he was arrested and placed in the Tower on suspicion of treason, more specifically of plotting to betray the town of Calais to the French. Although found not to have been involved, Arthur was kept in the Tower for two years, clearly because of Henry's anger. When he received news of his release in 1542, he had a heart attack and died. He is buried at the Tower of London.

Arthur married twice, firstly to Elizabeth Grey in 1511, who bore him three daughters. After her death he married Honor Grenville in 1529, a widow, with children from her previous marriage, whom Arthur helped raise.

De MARILLAC, Charles
(c.1510–1560)

French Ambassador at the English court between 1538 and 1543. His surviving letters give an insight into the goings on at the Tudor court.

NORTH, Edward
(c.1504–1564)

Clerk of the Parliament 1531–1541; Treasurer of the Court of Augmentations 1541–1547; High Sheriff of Cambridgeshire 1543; Sole Chancellor of the Court of Augmentations 1545–1547; Member of the Privy Council 1546.
North studied at St Paul's along with Wriothesley and Paget, before attending Peterhouse, Cambridge, and finishing his education in the Inns of Court. At the creation of the Court of Augmentations he was made its treasurer and worked closely with Rich in the dissolution of the monasteries, acquiring properties for himself. He would jointly hold the title of Chancellor with

Rich for a time until Rich left the court and North became sole Chancellor until he was forced to give the title up when Edward became king. When Audley resigned the office of Chancellor, North was sent, along with Thomas Pope, to collect the great seal and hand it to the king. In 1528 he married Alice Squire, who bore him two sons and two daughters. He married for the second time around 1561 to Margaret Butler

Under Queen Mary he rose in prominence again and re-entered the Privy Council. He was created Lord North of Kirtling in 1554. Under Elizabeth he continued to be held in high regard; she even held court at his mansion in the London Charterhouse for five days in November 1561. After this he retired from court life and died at his London home in 1546. He is buried at All Saints, Kirtling.

PAGET, William
(1505–1563)

Clerk of the Signet 1528; JP Middlesex 1536 and 1545; Clerk of the Privy Council 1540; Clerk of the Parliament 1541; Ambassador to the French Court 1541; Principal Secretary of State 1543; MP for Staffordshire 1547; Comptroller of the Household 1547; Chancellor of the Duchy of Lancaster 1547.

Paget was educated at St Paul's School, along with the likes of Wriothesley and Edward North, and then at Trinity Hall in Cambridge under Gardiner, before finishing his education at Gray's Inn. In 1530 he was sent with Edward Foxe and others to the University of Paris to discuss the king's marriage to Catherine of Aragon. Paget visited France numerous times in the 1530s on various diplomatic missions, during which time he established a network of spies and informants on the continent. He was appointed secretary to Jane Seymour, Anne of Cleves and Catherine Howard.

By the 1540s Paget was one of the most influential office holders in Henry's court. He became the middleman for those wishing to speak to the king, and for messages the king was sending out, making him a powerful man. He was the king's mouthpiece during the trial of the Earl of Surrey and made sure the verdict was what the king expected. After Henry died Paget was the man behind the scenes, making sure the king's final wishes were followed. He worked alongside Somerset and ensured that he was made protector instead of a body of councillors, setting in motion the power struggle over the following years.

Although he started to grow concerned at Somerset's poor judgement, he stood by him initially. When Somerset fell from power, Paget was with him and was tasked with arresting him. After this Paget surrendered his comptrollership, and his powerful position in the court gradually declined. He was accused of corruption in 1552. Under Mary he received a full pardon and was restored to the Privy Council, but she did not trust him. He was one of the principal members of her court in promoting the marriage to Phillip of Spain, and he argued that the monastic lands given out during the dissolution could not be returned to the Pope. Under Elizabeth he still played a part in court life, but his health had started to deteriorate. He died on 9/10 June 1563 and is buried at St Martins, West Drayton.

PAULET, William
(c.1488–1572)

MP for Hampshire 1529; Surveyor-General of Wards' and Widows' Lands *1531; Comptroller of the Household 1532–1537; Treasurer 1537–1530; Baron St John 1539; Master of the Court of Wards 1540 and 1542; Keeper of the Great Seal 1547; Earl of Wiltshire 1550; Lord Treasurer 1550–1572; Marquess of Winchester 1551.*

Not much detail of Paulet's earlier years is known, but he did study at the Inns of Court. Before that he was an apprentice in shire administration. In 1523 he was knighted and three years later made a councillor. He was with the Duke of Suffolk in 1533 when his household was ordered to be reduced, and in 1534 was one of the councillors sent to the Princess Mary to persuade her to renounce her title as princess.

Paulet made a career as a bureaucrat and member of the nobility under the Tudor monarchs. He was highly respected by Henry VIII and was made an executor of his will[1], placing him above Cranmer and the Chancellor.

In the mid-Tudor crisis, he initially supported Warwick over Somerset and was rewarded by being made Earl of Wiltshire and Lord Treasurer. He played his role so well that the following year he was promoted to marquess. Paulet continued to support Warwick when Mary claimed herself as queen, and as a result of this support was placed under house arrest, though his position was restored when Mary knew he could be trusted. For the rest of his life, he continued to serve the monarchs and was an active member of the court.

Paulet married Elizabeth Capell who bore him four daughters and four sons. He died on 10 March 1572 and is buried at St Mary's Church, Basing.

PETRE, William
(1505–1572)

Canon of Lincoln Cathedral 1536–7; MP for Essex 1536, 1547, 1553, 1554, 1555, 1558 and 1559; King's Councillor 1545–1572; Deputy Keeper of the Seal of the Duchy of Lancaster 1543–4; Junior Principal Secretary of State 1544–1557; Treasurer First Fruits and Tenths 1549–1553.

Petre entered Oxford as a student of law in 1519 and graduated in 1526. He was working as a chancery clerk by 1533. In 1536 was promoted to a mastership in Chancery and was appointed to study papal bulls. Petre was heavily involved in the dissolution of various religious houses between 1535 and 1540 but did so fairly with no reputation for being greedy or corrupt, unlike others carrying out the same role. He was devoted to his work and did not get embroiled in the politics of the court. He was appointed a minor assistant executor of Henry VIII's will and was the only one who did not receive anything from this. He was described later as being 'the man who said nothing[2]'. He served Cromwell and, later, Cecil while he was secretary to Somerset. Petre was with Somerset when he fled to Hampton Court with Edward VI in October 1549. Somerset sent Petre to London to speak with Warwick and the others, but rather than defending Somerset he was won over by their reasoning and changed his loyalties. Under Mary he was charged with restoring various religious statutes which Edward had altered in favour of the reformed religion and was also part of the negotiations of Mary's marriage to Phillip II. After Phillip had left England for good, Petre was be one of the men who kept him informed of what was happening.

He married Gerturde Tyrrell, and later Ann Brown, both from Essex, where he had created his principal seat in Ingatestone (which is still owned by his descendants today). He died on 13 January 1572 and is buried at St Edmunds and St Marys Church, Ingatestone.

PHILIP II of Spain
(1527–1598)

King of Spain 1556–1598; King of England (through marriage) 1554–1558. Philip was at times at odds with England due to opposing religious beliefs. He was staunchly Catholic and saw himself as defender of Catholic Europe. He was King of Spain during its golden age and ruled over a large part of Europe. He married Queen Mary I (his second marriage) in 1543 as a political alliance, although for Mary it was for love. Due to concerns by her counsellors, Mary agreed to adding terms to the marriage, limiting his power and influence in England. After her death he proposed a match with Elizabeth, which she refused. In 1558 he sent a large armada of ships to invade England and depose Elizabeth, but many of the ships were wrecked during a terrible storm. He married another two times after Mary, each producing children.

ROPER, Margaret (née MORE)
(c.1504–1544)

Eldest daughter of Thomas More, Margaret and her brothers and sisters were given an equally thorough education which led to her reputation for being intelligent and knowledgeable, which was uncommon at the time (unless one was a royal female). She was even invited to court to discuss the classics with the king. At the age of 19 she translated Erasmus's *Precatio Dominica*.

When her father was imprisoned in 1534, she visit regularly and wrote to him. She appealed for his release and wrote to Cromwell to ask that her father's living conditions be improved. After his execution she bribed an official to retrieve his head from Tower bridge in order to bury it (it was eventually buried with her). She collected her father's writings and documents, which she passed to her husband, William Roper, who wrote a biography of More. She died in 1544 and was initially buried at Chelsea Parish Church, later being reburied at St Dunstan's, Canterbury, along with her husband and his family. She bore five children, all of whom were educated by her.

ROPER, William
(c.1496–1578)

Lawyer, MP, and son-in-law to Thomas More. He wrote Thomas More's biography.

SADLER, Ralph
(1507–1587)

Gentleman of the King's Privy Chamber 1536; High Treasurer of the Army 1547; Chancellor of the Duchy of Lancaster 1568.
As a young boy, Sadler was placed in the household of Cromwell, where he was taken under his wing and given a decent education in languages as well as learning the law and finances. Their friendship continued and he was considered one of Cromwell's most trusted associates, acting in effect like his personal secretary. Known for his diplomatic skills, Sadler was sent on various missions to Scotland, the first in 1537 to investigate complaints made by the king's sister about her husband, King James V of Scotland.

Sadler survived Cromwell's fall, and remained at court. Under Mary, however, he retired, probably due to his religious beliefs. When Elizabeth came to the throne he returned to court and became one of Cecil's most trusted servants. He was, reluctantly, one of the commissioners appointed to deal with Mary, Queen of Scots, and even found himself her gaoler in 1572 and 1584.

He died on 30 March 1587. He was said to be the richest commoner in England, and was, it seems, trusted by many in the Tudor court.

SEYMOUR, Edward (Duke of Somerset)
(c.1500–1552)

1st Duke of Somerset 1547–1552; 1st Earl of Hertford 1537–1552; 1st Viscount Beauchamp 1536–1552 Lord High Admiral 1542–1543; Lord High Treasurer 1547–1549; Earl Marshall 1547–1540; Lieutenant of the Realm 1544; Lord Lieutenant of Berkshire 1551–1552; Lord Protector of England 1547–1549.
Brother to Jane Seymour and uncle to Edward VI, Somerset was a skilled politician, soldier and reformer, and popular with the general public. He was

knighted for his part in the Duke of Suffolk's campaign in France in 1523. He became very close to the king in his final years, which was made even easier after Henry Howard's downfall. His brother, Thomas, was jealous of his power and prominence, which led to them falling out. Thomas was eventually arrested and executed on the orders of Edward. Henry VIII had left instructions in his will for a group of men to govern the country until his son reached the age of 18, but Somerset managed to get the regency council to appoint him as Lord Protector, making him king in all but name. After uprisings in 1549 and 1549 Somerset's popularity with the nobility plummeted, and they plotted to have him removed from power. On hearing of this, Edward sent out a call for help to those still loyal to him, and took the young king to Windsor in October 1559, effectively as a hostage. He was arrested and placed in the Tower, but released the following year and allowed back onto the Privy Council. However, he was later sent to the Tower once more, before being executed for attempting to overthrow his replacement, John Dudley.

Edward married for the first time in 1518 to Catherine Fillol, who gave him two sons. However, Edward believed Catherine had been having an affair and disputed their parentage. His second marriage was to Anne Stanhope, who bore him 10 children. He is buried in St Peter ad Vincula.

SOUTHWELL, Richard
(1502–1564)

JP for Norfolk and Suffolk 1531–1554; Sheriff of Norfolk and Suffolk 1534; Receiver of the Court of Augmentations 1536–42; General Surveyor of the King's Lands 1542–1547; Knight of the Shire for Norfolk 1553–1556.

Hailing from a Norfolk family who were clients of the Howards. He entered Lincoln's Inn in 1526 and became a friend to Cromwell who employed him as a tutor to his son, Gregory.

In April 1532, Southwell was involved in the murder of Sir William Pennington in Westminster, but due to his with the Howards and Cromwell he was granted a pardon from the king. As Receiver of the Court of Augmentations, Southwell was responsible for dealing with the dissolved monasteries in East Anglia, where he himself acquired land. Although he had Catholic sympathies, he was involved in Thomas More's downfall, and was one of the men sent with Rich on that infamous day. At More's trial, Southwell is said to have claimed he did not hear the supposed conversation that took place, perhaps to avoid making an enemy of Rich and not to betray his conscience and condemn More.

He was knighted in 1540 and was one of those responsible for the condemning evidence which sent the Earl of Surrey to his death in 1546. When Henry VIII died in 1547, he was one of the named assistant executors of his will. His position in court under Edward would change with the change of power, and it was not until Mary came to the throne that he was restored to the Privy Council and made Master of the Ordnance. He married twice, which both produced daughters. Southwell died on 11 January 1564 and is buried at Woodrising Church.

Tilney, Agnes (The Dowager Duchess of Norfolk)
(c.1477–1545)

Agnes Tilney became the second wife of Thomas Howard, 2nd Duke of Norfolk, on 17 August 1497 and bore him 10 children, including William Howard, 1st Baron Howard of Effingham, and Lord Thomas Howard. As Thomas rose in the court of Henry VII and Henry VIII so too did Agnes. She was godmother to Princess Mary and served a number of Henry's queens, two of whom were her step-grandchildren. Thomas died in 1522 and Agnes never remarried.

Things turned against Agnes in autumn 1541 when Cranmer was made aware of Queen Catherine Howard's potential affair, and in November members of the dowager's household were arrested and questioned. As events unfolded, her stepson, the Duke of Norfolk, turned his back on her as it became apparent that she had tried to destroy evidence. Due to her age and frailty, she was never placed on trial but was imprisoned and made to forfeit her land and goods. The king wanted her to be arrested for treason but was persuaded not to. She was eventually released and died in May 1545. She is buried in St Mary's Church, Lambeth, Surrey.

WINGFIELD, Anthony
(c.1488–1552)

Esquire of the Body 1508; Chief Steward to the Duke of Suffolk 1515; Sheriff of Norfolk and Suffolk 1515–16; Commissioner for Valuing Religious Houses 1536; Privy Councillor 1539; Vice-Chamberlain of the household 1547–1550; Comptroller of the Household 1550; Exchequer Chamberlain 1550.

A soldier and administrator, from a prominent family in Suffolk, Anthony rose in the royal household and was a close friend to Charles Brandon. He became captain of the guard in 1539 and held the position the following year when Cromwell was arrested. He was one of the men who escorted Cromwell to the Tower. On Henry VIII's death Wingfield was named an assistant counsellor of his will. He backed Warwick in the power struggle between Warwick and Somerset and was sent to Windsor to arrest Somerset when he attempted to gain control over the young king in 1549. In 1551, along with Rich, he was sent as an emissary to Lady Mary in an attempt to get her to convert. He married Elizabeth Vere and the union produced at least 10 children. He died on 15 August 1552 and is buried in Stepney.

WOLSEY, Thomas
(c.1473–1530)

Master of Magdalen College; Rector of St Mary's Church, Limington 1500–1509; Chaplain to Archbishop of Canterbury 1502–3; Archbishop of York 1514–1530; Canon of Windsor 1511; Bishop of Lincoln 1514; Bishop of London 1515; Bishop of Bath and Wells 1518–1529; Prince-bishop of Durham 1523–1529; Bishop of Winchester 1529–1530; Lord Chancellor 1515–1529.

Despite his humble beginnings, Wolsey rose to become the second most powerful man in England after King Henry VIII. He fell from power after failing to grant the king a divorce from Catherine of Aragon. Knowing he was in danger, he went to his power base in York, hoping to keep his head down and focus on his ecclesiastical duties. He was charged with treason and died on the way to London to face trial. Wolsey never married but did have a mistress, Joan Larke, with whom he had two children.

Wriothesley, Thomas (Earl of Southampton)
(1505–1550)

1st Earl of Southampton 1547–1550; Secretary of State 1540–1544; Lord Chancellor 1544–1547; MP for Hampshire 1539 and 1542; Ambassador to the Queen of Hungary 1538–1539; Keeper of the Great Seal 1544; Baron Wriothesley 1544–1550; Member of Edward VI's Regency Council 1547.
A member of the Catholic faction in the Tudor court, Thomas was a skilled politician and loyal to Henry VIII. He allied himself with several Catholic nobles, including Gardiner, and attempted to bring about the downfall of Kathryn Parr through her ladies. He was actively involved in the illegal torture of Anne Askew, along with Rich. He was dismissed from his place on the Regency Council but still held some influence and was involved in Edward Seymour's downfall. He is buried in St Peter's Church, Titchfield.

WYATT, Thomas
(c.1503–1542)

High Marshal at Calais 1528–1530; High Sheriff of Kent 1536; MP for Kent December 1541.
A politician, ambassador and poet, Wyatt is credited with introducing the sonnet to English literature. Born in Allington Castle, Kent, he knew the Boleyn family growing up and was close to Anne Boleyn. He entered court life as Sewer Extraordinary and his life in the Tudor court progressed from there. In 1526 he accompanied Sir John Russell to Rome to petition the Pope to annul Henry VIII's marriage to Catherine of Aragon. He was arrested in 1536 for allegedly having been intimate with Anne Boleyn. He was imprisoned in the Tower but eventually released as a result of his friendship with Cromwell. He married Elizabeth Brook in 1520 and one of their children, Thomas Wyatt the younger, was responsible for Wyatt's Rebellion in 1554. In 1541 he was arrested once more, this time surviving thanks to the involvement of Catherine Howard. He died on 11 October 1542 and is buried in Sherborne Abbey.

Notes

Introduction

1. Campbells lives of chancellors
2. Meyer, 208
3. Hugh Trevor-Roper, Historian
4. Dasent, 1911
5. Summers, 2015
6. Stone, 1968

The Life and Career of Richard Rich

1. Pollard, 1896
2. Carter, 2004
3. Will of John Rich 1509: 'England & Wales, Prerogative Court of Canterbury Wills, 1384–1858', The National Archives; Kew, Surrey, England; Records of the Prerogative Court of Canterbury, Series PROB 11; Class: PROB 11; Piece: 16
4. Bindoff, 1982 Richard Rich
5. Carter, 2004
6. ibid
7. Dury, 1990
8. A dwelling house together with its outbuildings, curtilage, and the adjacent land appropriated to its use (Collins dictionary)
9. Simpson, W. Sparrow (1870). The Journal of the British Archaeological Association. London: British Archaeological Association. pp.161–3
10. Kelly, 2012
11. Thin, soft silk with a slight sheen.
12. L&P Volume 9, 114–133
13. Kelly, 2012
14. Borman, 2015
15. Carter, 2003
16. L&P V. 14 Pt 2
17. Samantha Bullat, historical tailor and dress historian
18. This is just an estimate
19. Baker, 1986
20. ibid p.9
21. BL, Harley MS 1042, fol. 47v.
22. L&P V.4 November 1528, 11–20
23. Bindoff, 1982, Richard Rich
24. ibid
25. Webb, 1921
26. Bindoff, 1982 Richard Rich
27. Justices of the Peace Act 1361

28. Lander, 1986 p2
29. L&P, V.11, p257–284.
30. L&P V.5, p415–430.
31. Horowitz, 2011
32. Bindoff, 1982 Richard Rich
33. Solomon was a king of Israel known for his wisdom, Samson, legendary Israelite warrior and judge, or divinely inspired leader, renowned for the prodigious strength.
34. Bindoff, 1982 Richard Rich
35. Clark, 1990 p68
36. Bindoff, 1982 Richard Rich
37. Third Report of the Deputy Keeper of the Public Records (1842) p226
38. Edwards, 2001 p98
39. Lipscomb, 2009 p26
40. Vaughn, 1958
41. Lotherington, 2004 p134
42. Strype, 1816
43. see Whos Who
44. see Whos Who
45. 24 Hen. VIII, c. 12; 27 Hen. VIII, c. 27
46. Richardson, 1961
47. Lipscomb, 2015

The Trial of Thomas More

1. Guy, 1976
2. L&P V.7, p114–126
3. Ackroyd, 1999 p350
4. Rogers, 1947
5. Sylvester, 1962 p246
6. Paul, 2025 p419
7. William Roper – Hitchcock, 1958
8. Ackroyd, 1999 p379–80
9. Russell, 2018
10. Transcr. Statutes of the Realm, iii. 508.
11. Salmon, 1719
12. Sargent, 1936
13. Howell, 1816
14. ibid
15. Harpsfield, 2020 p54–8
16. Sargent, 1970 p7
17. Thomas, 1999 p156

The Dissolution and the Court of Augmentations

1. (27 Hen. 8) C A P. XXVIII
2. MacCulloch, 2018
3. L&P V.15 p21–30
4. Loades, 1968 p159–60
5. L&P V.11, p595–6
6. Richardson, 1961 p5
7. XXVII The statutes of the realm v3
8. Richardson, 1961

9. L&P V.16, p350–365
10. Colvin, 1975 p40
11. Doc 25 Section VIII
12. Younings, 1971, p120
13. Richardson, 1971, p296
14. L&P V.5, p619–636
15. L&P V.9, p1–19
16. L&P V.11, p2–19
17. L&P V.11 p591–593
18. L&P V.11, p114–129
19. L&P V.12 Part 1, p399–433
20. Richardson, 1971 p310
21. ibid
22. L&P V. 14 Part 2 p170–176
23. Elton, 1969 p215
24. L&P V.10, p424–440
25. L&P V.12 Part 1, p1–16
26. Arthur Plantagenet, 1st Viscount Lisle and his wife Elizabeth.
27. L&P V.11, p103–114
28. L&P V.11, p157–175
29. L&P V. 11, p157–175
30. L&P V.11, p541–547
31. L&P V. 12 Part 2, p228–245
32. ibid p245–262
33. ibid p324–335
34. Richardson, 1971 p8
35. ibid p8
36. Clark, 1990 p68
37. Nicolas, 1834 p169
38. Richardson, 1971 p.27
39. ibid p28
40. he established himself a large estate in Essex, this is discussed in chapter 10
41. Clark, 1990 p68
42. L&P V.12 Part 1 p584–607
43. L&P Volume 13 Part 1, p223–250
44. ibid V.14 Part 1,p399–424
45. ibid v15 p325–349
46. ibid v17 p199–218
47. ibid v.17 p245–6
48. ibid v18 p510
49. ibid v21 p1 p123–153
50. Borman, 2015
51. CSP 8 (i) 178
52. Borman, 2015 p333–4
53. Stone, 1966

The Downfall of Thomas Cromwell

1. Sir John Wallop, a diplomat in Henry VIII court
2. L&P V. 9, p288–310
3. Overseeing the Crown Jewels which were housed at the Tower of London.

4. Elton, 196,9 p97
5. Borman, 2015, pp2–3
6. ibid p52
7. Dickens 1964, p37
8. Elton, 1969, p85
9. L&P V.11
10. L&P V.11, p492–513
11. L&P V.11, p221–257
12. L&P V.14 Part 2, p196–208
13. ibid V.15, p1–19
14. Wier, 2007, p417
15. ibid
16. Borman, 2015, p530
17. ibid
18. ibid p531
19. Hutchinson, 2014 p1
20. L&P V.15 p376–412
21. Where Anne Boleyn and later her daughter were held. The building no longer exists but were located just in front of the White Tower
22. L&P V. XV: 804
23. Bindoff, 1982 Richard Rich
24. L&P Volume XV p376–412
25. Kaulek [189] [London,] 11
26. Hutchinson, 2005, p97
27. MacCulloch, 1996, p270
28. L&P V. 15, p364
29. Angus, 2021
30. Baldwin-Smith, 1954
31. His fall was after Cromwell's execution
32. Baldwin Smith, 1954
33. L&P V.16, p284
34. Borman, 2015
35. L&P V.15, p436–445
36. SP V.viii. p. 545.
37. L&P V.16, p219–229
38. L&P V. 15, p203

After Cromwell: Factions and Torture

1. L&P V.16, p644–660
2. Russel, 2018 p156
3. L&P V. 16, p660–671
4. Plowden, 2002, p102
5. Jones, 2011, p202
6. Russell, 2012, p301
7. For more on interrogation techniques used in the Tudor ages see Carlton, Charles. 'Thomas Cromwell: A Study in Interrogation'. Albion: A Quarterly Journal Concerned with British Studies, vol. 5, no. 2, 1973, pp. 116–27. JSTOR,
8. L&P V.16, p660-671
9. ibid

10. ibid V. 16, p644–660
11. ibid
12. ibid
13. Wriothesley Volume 1.
14. The offence of concealing knowledge of a felony (or treason) by one who has not participated or assisted in it but does not report it to a proper authority [Collins dictionary]
15. L&P V.16, p681–696
16. Wriothesley V.1 p.132
17. L&P V. p644–660
18. ibid V.19 Part 1, p141–178
19. ibid V.17, p706-712
20. Bindoff, 1982 Richard Rich
21. L&P V.xix pt1 p370
22. Richardson, 1961, p66
23. Bindoff, 1982 Richard Rich
24. L&P V. 19 Part 2, pp36–54
25. ibid V. 19 Part 2, p103–114
26. ibid V.19 Part 2
27. ibid
28. National archives currency converter
29. L&P V. 19 Part 2, p215–234
30. ibid
31. L&P V. 19 Part 2, p234–249
32. ibid V.19 Part 2, p272–321
33. ibid v.19 Part 2, p458–478
34. ibid V. 20 Part 1
35. Along with Lord St. John, Chamberlain of the Household, Sir Richard Southwell, one of the General Surveyors and John Wynter, paymaster of the King's ships.
36. L&P V. 20 Part 2
37. NA Currency converter
38. L&P V.19 Part 1, p358–388
39. Hutchinson, 2014
40. Jardine, 2024 p15
41. Foxe, 2011
42. ibid
43. ibid
44. ibid
45. ibid
46. ibid
47. ibid
48. see Whos Who
49. L&P xxi. Part 2. p364
50. He would remain in the Tower of London until August 1553, when Mary came to the throne.
51. NA currency convertor
52. L&P V.21 Part 2, p313–348

Lord Chancellor

1. Nichols, 1857
2. Fitzroy, 1928, pp62–3

3. Wilson, 2005 p181
4. Elton, 1969, p 312
5. Wier, 2008 p399
6. L&P V. 19 Part 1, p1–17
7. L&P V.19 Part 1,p288–296
8. For the sentence against Wriothesley see the Privy Council Book in the Public Record office [PRO], PC2/2, fols. 105 and 186–190.
9. ibid
10. He was initially buried in London but was later reburied in Titchfield.
11. 1 Edward VI, c. 11
12. Bindoff, 1982 Richard Rich
13. ibid
14. Nichols, 1996, p288
15. Porter, 2009, p177
16. Nichols, 1857
17. ibid
18. Porter, 2009, p177
19. ibid p182
20. https://archive.org/stream/originallettersi02elliuoft#page/178/mode/2up, p. 179–182. You can see photos of the original letter on the National Archives website at http://www.nationalarchives.gov.uk/education/resources/the-english-reformation-c1527-1590/mary-writes-to-edward-vi/
21. Wriothesley, 1857, p2 pp33–4
22. Foxe, 2011
23. Pollard, 1965, p261
24. Loades, 1994, p34
25. Wriothesley, 1875, pp25–6
26. Loades 2004, p.110
27. A note on this point regarding his involvement in Thomas Mores downfall, he was not the one who was trying More, just the man giving the evidence.
28. Nichols, 1857, p347
29. Edward VI, Chronicle, 84–85: Oct. 2, 1551
30. CSP xiii pg 36
31. Campbell, 2019
32. Fuller's Church History, 1665, I. 408.
33. ibid
34. Some records mention a rumour was going around saying Rich had planned to give it to Somerset somehow.
35. APC iv, 277
36. Pollard, 1965, pp252–3
37. ibid 263–4
38. Loads, 1994, p83
39. Loades, 1996, p193
40. Skidmore, 2008, p248
41. MS. Petyt 47, f. 317.
42. Tallis, 2017, p146
43. MacCulloch, 1996, p544
44. Plowden, 2016
45. MS. Petyt 47, f. 316

46. MS. Petyt 47, f. 316. Spelling adjusted to modern.
47. Ives, 2009
48. Loades, 1996
49. Foxe, 2011 book 10
50. it was signed by Cranmer, Suffolk, Petre, Arundel and others. Appendix Letter LXIX Strype
51. Stow, 1908 p67
52. Nichols, 1850 p7
53. Ives, 2009 p118
54. Loades, 1996, p222–3

Religion and Richard Rich

1. APC. iv, 300.
2. APC 318
3. APC 347
4. Foxe, 2011 p331
5. Wilson, 2005, p231
6. Thomas, 2019, p230
7. APC 335
8. John Bourchier
9. Sir Richard Morgan
10. APC 333
11. ibid 339
12. See further in this chapter for more on this
13. Bindoff, 1982 Richard Rich
14. ibid
15. It was the norm for younger daughters to join Syon Abbey before its destruction in the dissolution
16. Richards, 2009
17. SSP vii p54
18. ibid 4, p395
19. To be more precise they were first cousins, once removed. Phillips father was nephew to Katherine of Aragon, Marys mother.
20. Today this is known as Wyatts rebellion, led by Thomas Wyatt the Younger, Sir James Croft, Sir Peter Carew and Henry Grey – Duke of Suffolk. Due to lack of support, it failed, and its leaders were executed.
21. CSP Jan 1554
22. ibid v 2
23. ibid v3, p59
24. Mary's third parliament sat from 12 November 1554 through to 16 January 1555
25. House of Commons Journal Volume 1: 19 April 1554
26. Edwards, 2013, p265
27. Ridley, 2001, p80
28. Bindoff, 1982 Richard Rich
29. APC V. 5, p 104
30. ibid p140–1
31. ibid
32. Muller, 1926, p281–2
33. Foxe, 2011, 7, p123
34. ibid

35. ibid
36. Duffy, 2010, pp119–20
37. There is a memorial plaque in Rayleigh high street remembering Causton and John Ardley, who were burned at the stake in Rayleigh, along with remembering Robert Drakes and William Tyms, who were burned at Smithfield.
38. APC 5 148
39. Bindoff, 1982 Edmund Tyrell
40. ibid
41. ibid
42. ibid Richard Rich
43. APC p237
44. Foundation Deed of the Rich Chantry, 26 April 1555

The Last Years of Richard Rich

1. see who's who
2. William was appointed Secretary of State and a close confident and friend of Elizabeth whom she trusted. There was nothing going on in her court that he did not know about
3. Clark, 1990
4. National Archieves currency converter
5. APC v7 p17
6. ibid V6 p245
7. Clark, 1990
8. This is just my viewpoint – there is no evidence to corroborate this
9. The question of Elizabeth's marriage was a constant one during her reign, with various suitors being suggested and courted. She never married, and historians have various opinions as to why she did not do so.
10. The question of Elizabeth's marriage was a constant one during her reign, with various suitors being suggested and courted. She never married, and historians have various opinions as to why she did not do so.
11. Modern History Sourcebook: Queen Elizabeth I of England Selected Writing and Speeches
12. CSPA P212
13. Bindoff, 1982 Richard Rich
14. Ridley, 2001, p215
15. Statutes of the Realm, IV, 350 f.: I Elizabeth, c. I.
16. Guy, 1991, p264
17. Morant, 1786, p420
18. Strype, 1853
19. The almshouse, which Rich founded in 1565, is where Collyer's is located today. It was a timber-framed thatched structure, with a barn and a brewhouse attached. It burnt down in 1876 and was rebuilt a few years later in 1878.
20. Telfer, 1989
21. A 16th century clothier and diartest. He documented a number of events in his diary which covered 1550–1563
22. Machyn, 1848
23. ERO D/DP O40/1
24. Craze, 1955
25. Hoak, 1995, p183
26. Drury, 1990

27. He was a moral philosopher known primarily for his work in normative ethics, as well as in medical ethics.
28. Although there were accusations of being corrupt, they never progressed enough for Rich to have felt in danger

The Rich Family

1. This was the third creation with the previous two dying out, the first in 1499 and the second in 1590
2. Metcalf, 1878, p132
3. ibid
4. Nichols, 1857
5. L&P v.11, p349–378
6. Metcalf, 1878, p132
7. ibid
8. ibid
9. Bindoff, 1982 R. Drury
10. Bulwer, 1895 vol.2 p219
11. Metcalf, 1878, p132
12. Bindoff, 1982, R. Peyton
13. Metcalf, 1878, p132
14. Bindoff, 1982 R North
15. Metcalf, 1878, p132
16. Metcalf, 1878
17. ibid
18. ibid
19. Stone, 1965, p231–2
20. ibid
21. CSP p620
22. Stone, 1965, p231
23. Kelsey, 2004
24. ibid
25. ibid
26. Donagan, 2018
27. Thrush, 2010 H. Rich
28. ERO D/DP O40/1
29. Parish register of St Marys
30. Sidney,1896 v.48
31. Willis, Browne (1750). Notitia Parliamentarian, Part II: A Series or Lists of the Representatives in the several Parliaments held from the Reformation 1541 to the Restoration 1660, London, pp229–39.
32. Thrush, 2010 N. Rich
33. Shaw, 1906 p167
34. ibid
35. J. Foster, The Register of Admissions to Gray's Inn, 1521–1887
36. J.H. Lefroy, Memorials of the Discovery and Settlement of the Bermudas or Somers Islands 1511–1687, 2 Vols (Longmans, Green & Co., London 1879), II, pp. 122–23
37. Foster, John (1889). The Register of Admissions to Gray's Inn, 1521–1887
38. Gentles, 2004 N. Rich

Richard Rich and Essex

1. Bernard, 92, p153
2. Nicholson, 2012, ppx-xi
3. Ridley, 2002, p456
4. Girovard, 1978, p3
5. Son of Mary Boleyn and nephew of Anne. There are some who believe he could be the illegitimate child of Mary and Henry VIII, although this is unlikely. Other manors included Foulness, Nasewick, Arendells Marsh, Newewycke, Estwyke and Southwycke
6. NA currency converter
7. L&P v.10, p402–420
8. Essex Garden Trust
9. ibid
10. L&P v.13 Part, pp223–250
11. Although this is not certain
12. Morant 1768, ii, 845
13. Powell, 1983 vol 8, pp158–186
14. Lord Treasurer of England
15. Clark, 1990
16. Powell, 1983 v6, pp322–327
17. Ibid

Richard Rich in Screen and Print

1. Samson, 2010 Heartstone pg 547
2. https://www.pbs.org/wgbh/masterpiece/specialfeatures/the-characters-of-wolf-hall-the-mirror-and-the-light

The Greatest Tudor Villain?

1. Ridely 2001, p78

Who's' Who

1. He would be awarded £500 from Henrys will.
2. This was said by Gaspard de Coligny during the negotiations of the return of Boulogne, which Petre was a part of, in 1550.

Index